...melt...

...melt...

a book of chocolate

Louise Nason • Chika Watanabe
Photography by Jean Cazals

First published in Great Britain
in 2011 by

Absolute Press
Scarborough House
29 James Street West
Bath BA1 2BT
Phone 44 (0) 1225 316013
Fax 44 (0) 1225 445836
E-mail info@absolutepress.co.uk
Website www.absolutepress.co.uk

Publisher
Jon Croft
Commissioning Editor
Meg Avent
Art Director
Matt Inwood
Editor
Jane Middleton
Art Direction
Matt Inwood and Jean Cazals
Design
Matt Inwood and Claire Siggery
Photographer
Jean Cazals
Food Stylists
Louise Nason and Chika Watanabe

A catalogue record of this book is
available from the British Library.

ISBN 9781906650384

Printed and bound in Slovenia on behalf
of Latitude Press

A note about the text
This book is set in Helvetica Neue
and Modern No. 20. Helvetica was
designed in 1957 by Max Miedinger of
the Swiss-based Haas foundry. In the
early 1980s, Linotype redrew the entire
Helvetica family. The result was
Helvetica Neue. Modern No. 20 was
originally issued by the Stephenson
Blake foundry in 1905. Edouard
Benguiat recreated and updated the
font in the mid-1900s.

(L–R) Louise Nason; Chika Watanabe; Jean Cazals.

...contents...

...FOREWORD...

The name Melt was conceived over a blissful meal one balmy summer evening at the River Café in London. I was searching for a word used in chocolate terminology as well as one having good associations, and the word melt does just that.

•••

Chocolate, which melts at body temperature, should dissolve in your mouth in a silky mass, exploding with different flavours. A complex food with over 400 flavour notes, at its best it can provide an overwhelming taste sensation, lingering in your mouth long after the chocolate has melted away. At worst it can be cloying, sickly and sweet – but this is not what chocolate should be. Always hunt down the best. Bars should be of excellent quality, well made and stored at the right temperature and chocolates should be fresh.

•••

Melt was created two years after my fourth child was born and has almost become an extra member of my family. Its character is bright, excitable, spontaneous and it certainly has an interesting future.
We have a strong ethos and we follow the same principles that I use when cooking for my family at home: get the best raw ingredients, never compromise, and make sure everything is fresh.

Melt is the antithesis of corporate, which gives us the opportunity to be truly creative. Recipes can be inspired by a mood, a person, an encounter, or a chat with a customer. With excellent ingredients, skill, experience and imagination, our chocolatiers are able to create wonderfully innovative chocolates and bars.

•••

But you can create wonderful chocolates at home too. With this book, you can flip between easy domestic recipes and those that require a bit more skill and patience. Chocolate can be fairly tricky to master, but never fear, the beauty is that there is no waste. If your chocolate doesn't temper properly the first time, just melt it down and start again.

•••

Use this book to inspire and experiment, to practise and gain confidence and, best of all, to have fun and enjoy the whole chocolate-making (and eating!) process as much as we do. And if you are anywhere near our shop in London, do pop in and see us – we'd love to meet you!

•••

LOUISE NASON, Founder of Melt
August 2011

...foreword...

...tasting, eating and cooking with chocolate...

by Louise Nason

...DOES HIGHER COCOA CONTENT MEAN BETTER CHOCOLATE?...

The more cocoa content chocolate has, the nearer it is to real chocolate, but not necessarily chocolate as many people know it. Growing up in Britain in the 1980s, I was quite happy with a sweet, vaguely chocolatey taste of around 25–30 per cent cocoa solids. Since the late 1990s, cocoa content has become the only indication of quality that we look for on a bar of chocolate. Of course, it is rather more complex than that. Chocolate with a higher cocoa content is essential for cooking, giving cakes and desserts a richer, stronger taste, but it's important not to be fooled into thinking that a higher cocoa content automatically equals better flavour and quality when choosing chocolate for eating. This would be like going to a wine merchant and selecting only the bottles with the highest alcohol content. Cocoa percentage is just one of many indications of quality. Do, however, keep within the boundary of over 60 per cent cocoa solids for dark chocolate and 30 per cent cocoa solids for milk chocolate.

Technically, white chocolate is not in fact chocolate, as it does not contain any cocoa solids. It does, however, contain cocoa butter. One of the very few that I would eat is by a company called Felchlin, which produces what is called a non-deodorised white chocolate. It has a very slight lemony hint and is really lovely as it is not overly sweet.

Other factors affecting the quality of chocolate vary from bean type, provenance, terroir and numerous fascinating processing steps, right through to how the chocolatier tempers the chocolate and carefully matches different chocolates to different recipes. There are up to 15 complex steps in processing chocolate – fermentation, for example, is essential to bring out the chocolate flavour of the bean. Just after the seeds have been taken out of the pod, they are laid in oak fermenting boxes and left to ferment for approximately five days. Moving and loading the beans in the boxes can be backbreaking work. Banana leaves (amongst other things) are used to cover them, and oxidation and the breakdown of proteins into amino acids occur. Although the farmers are paid more for the fermented beans, known as hispaniola, this delicate and time-consuming process can be aborted too early if a farmer needs to enter the cocoa market quickly in order to sell beans when the price is highest. Reducing the fermentation period results in lower-quality cocoa. This is just one example of how the delicate process of making chocolate can be affected.

...WHAT IS FINE CHOCOLATE?...

Just under 5 per cent of the world's cocoa production is categorised as 'fine', meaning cocoa produced from the superior Criollo or Trinitario beans. The other main bean type, Forestero, which is hardy but lacking in flavour, accounts for 'bulk' or 'commercial' chocolate. With 70 per cent of the market coming from West Africa, these are really quite astounding statistics.

Cocoa is often considered a poor man's crop by farmers. They are keen to diversify in order to minimise their losses, since not only can there all too frequently be a low price for their beans but the cocoa tree doesn't start to produce pods until it is about five years' old. Add the fact that the crop is often blighted by diseases and the farmer very often has to cultivate other crops, such as rubber. In the Caribbean, bananas tend to be the farmers' primary cash crop, with cocoa secondary.

However, there are currently some interesting developments in the world of chocolate, as chocolatiers and chefs with a passion for the product and an obsession with excellence embark on a mission to find really high-quality chocolate. One way to do this is via 'bean to bar' craftsmanship – which means that the maker of the bar of chocolate sources the chocolate, maybe even owning the plantation, and maintains contact with the product right through all the processes to finished point of sale. This ensures a level of control and quality that is very unusual in the history of chocolate manufacturing. Sourcing a particular bean from a known plantation and controlling and nurturing its journey gives the customer many assurances – the main one being at source point, where the chocolate maker will have a good relationship with the cocoa farmers and pay them a fair price for their beans.

The future of chocolate farming needs to be looked after carefully. Bodies such as the International Cocoa Organisation (ICCO) and World Cocoa Foundation (WCF) are doing excellent work – ICCO's mandate being 'to work towards a sustainable world cocoa economy' that encompasses social, economic and environmental dimensions in both production and consumption.

I believe the 'bean to bar' development is the most exciting and empowering one to date – and in some cases should even be termed 'tree to bar'. At Melt we have been using such a chocolate for many years, made by the Colombian company, Santander. It has built up a strong community through growing, processing and manufacturing chocolate on site. Another inspiring company is the Grenada Chocolate Company, founded by Mott Green. He is as passionate about reviving cocoa growing as he is about creating good, secure jobs for the local community. Under this set up, he has enabled fantastic-tasting dark chocolate to be made in a socially responsible way – even the factory is solar-powered. This is where the most interesting future for chocolate lies.

15

...tasting, eating and cooking with chocolate...

...CHOCOLATE SHOULD BE ENJOYED EVERY DAY!...

Everything in moderation – it may sound dull but it is certainly true. Chocolate, coffee and wine are delightful stimulants, best enjoyed with quality, not quantity, in mind. You will get far more satisfaction – and greater health benefits – from a small piece of top-quality chocolate than from a greasy, insipid-looking '2 for 1' bar of low-cocoa-content confectionery. If the chocolate is cheap, you really have to bear in mind what the farmers will have received for their beans at the beginning of the chain.

16 Here is the polar explorer, Ranulph Fiennes, on the benefits of chocolate: 'Chocolate keeps you going medically when on the ice ... without a square every few minutes, hypothermia and hypoglycaemia set in.' Dark chocolate contains some key nutrients, with the all-important and pleasurable 'feel-good' factor coming from phenylethylamine, plus other heath-giving properties from cocoa flavonoids, which are powerful anti-oxidants. Cocoa butter is also rich in good fats, equivalent to the fats found in nuts and avocados. Why do you think the precious cocoa butter is sometimes removed and sold separately? Watch out for this trick – in lower-quality chocolate the cocoa fat may have been extracted and sold for a good sum to the cosmetic industry, while the remaining cocoa solids are combined with cheap vegetable fats, which spoil the taste. Always check the label of the chocolate before buying.

When you buy chocolate for eating rather than cooking, smell it before you taste it. Smell is responsible for approximately 80 per cent of our taste. I tend to eat less chocolate when I am working at Melt, as I find the sheer intoxicating aroma satisfying in itself. The smell of decent chocolate should be like a good-quality wine or perfume – clean, distinct and natural, with no cloying or artificial notes. Above all, it should not have the smell of fatty, sickly sweetness that confectionery (i.e. chocolate with a cocoa content of under 30 per cent) has. There may be a long 'finish' to the chocolate, which is wonderful and a real treat if those strong chocolate notes go on and on, but beware of any artificial aftertaste or cloying quality. For cooking, if you take care over your ingredients, you will enjoy a better chocolate, or a better dessert, as the quality will shine through.

Chocolate is probably the best-loved flavour in the world. Although it has undergone major developments through the centuries, it has always been categorised as a mood-enhancing food, sometimes even as an aphrodisiac. From medicinal roots to what is commonly considered today as everyone's pick-me-up of choice, chocolate really is the most wonderful food to cook with and to eat. So make sure you enjoy the best chocolate you can buy.

...WHEN IS THE BEST TIME TO EAT CHOCOLATE?...

Well frankly, any time that takes your fancy! I particularly like to taste chocolate for work in the morning, when my tastebuds are most receptive. I feel I can make a better judgement then rather than later in the day when I might be influenced by hunger. Tasting chocolate in the morning also reminds me of happy times: Christmas, Easter, birthdays, all the times I ate chocolate in the morning as a child; celebration indeed for the tastebuds!

Generally dark chocolate is good in the morning, strong and intense like an espresso. Your newly awakened tastebuds will really be able to seek out all the complex chocolate notes to be found. Milk chocolate is ideal to help satisfy the afternoon energy dip, and you could then enjoy a small amount of dark chocolate after dinner – to 'finish' the meal.

...TO SWEETEN AND FLAVOUR OR NOT?...

The Mayans ate plenty of honey with their chocolate, so chocolate has historically been sweetened. However, if you make good dark chocolate, you need less sugar, so you can allow the natural flavour notes to sing through. As a consequence, dark chocolate is more nutritious. Most people find it very difficult to eat as much dark chocolate as they might milk chocolate, in any case.

There is also the debate amongst chocolate aficionados as to whether vanilla should be added to chocolate as a matter of course. Again, vanilla has been a component of chocolate drinks for centuries, to make them more palatable. This is not such an issue if the vanilla is of good quality and natural, but do steer away from any chocolate containing artificial vanillin, as it will mask the natural notes within the chocolate and may interfere with the aftertaste.

...tasting, eating and cooking with chocolate...

...EXPLORE THE WORLD OF CHOCOLATE...

The sheer volume and variety of chocolate available can be quite overwhelming. Customers come into Melt and whisper under their breath, apologising for their liking for milk chocolate. Yet milk chocolate is wonderful, and especially satisfying in cold weather. If you give yourself time, dark chocolate can also be wonderful, but your tastebuds may just need to be tuned into its intensity. Look out for red fruit notes, caramel undertones and earthy qualities in the chocolate you try – you'll be surprised! Everyone's tastebuds and taste memories are different, so take a little time to discover your favourite flavours and savour what you choose.

Create a tasting event for yourself by buying several bars of chocolate, ranging from the cheapest milk chocolate with under 30 per cent cocoa content through to the darkest you can find. Invite around a few friends and make an evening of it (see 'What to drink with chocolate', page 21).

Opposite is a selection of chocolate bars that are readily available from major supermarkets and other shops. This will give you a broad range and a good start towards identifying the different flavours, textures and tastes that the world of chocolate can yield.

Milka Alpine Milk

This contains vegetable fat – can you detect it? Do you find it affects the texture and taste? This chocolate also contains the artificial flavouring, vanillin: do you find this interferes or lingers as an aftertaste?

Green & Black's Milk Chocolate

No vegetable fat in this one, just pure cocoa butter, which is more expensive to produce, but vital for the right 'melt' and taste. It contains natural, organic vanilla, so try to really appreciate the better-quality ingredients in this chocolate, which has 34 per cent cocoa solids.

Lindt Excellence 70% Cocoa

After the milk chocolate you will really notice the increased cocoa content here – this is getting more like real chocolate! It is certainly chocolatey, but a little neutral for expanding your flavour bank.

Valrhona Grand Cru Caraïbe Dark Chocolate

Really concentrate: you should get a much more distinct, cleaner flavour profile. It is made solely from Trinitario beans from the Caribbean and so is known as a single-estate chocolate.

This example illustrates that cocoa content does not always equate to quality. It has a lower cocoa content (66 per cent) than the previous bar but significantly superior qualities. Note the length of flavour – the taste of chocolate should linger in your mouth for a good couple of minutes. Concentrate on the young, lively, fruity notes, followed by the subtle flavour of roasted nuts.

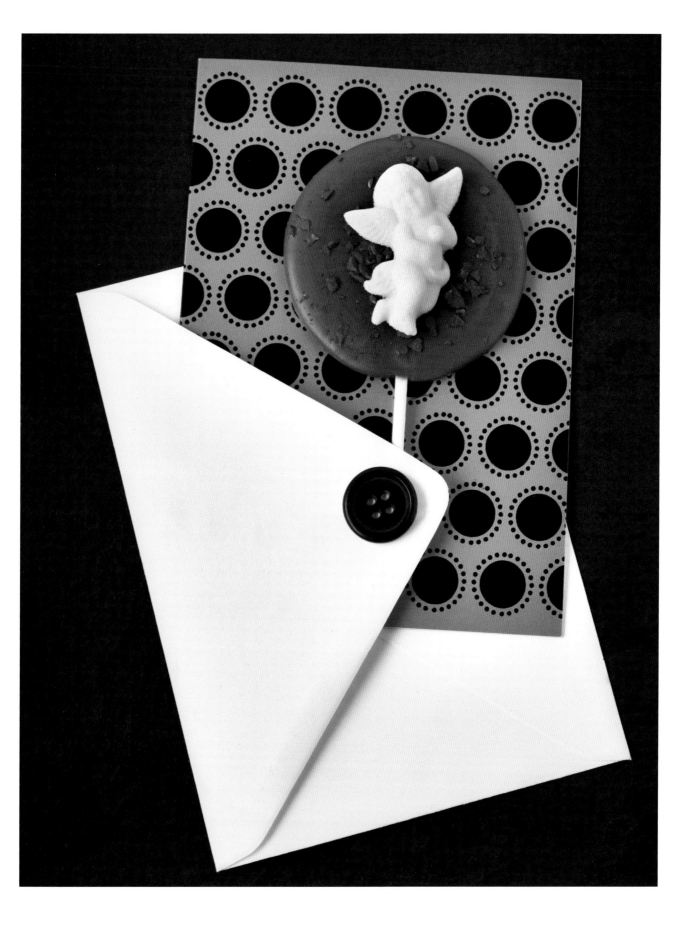

...WHAT TO DRINK WITH CHOCOLATE...

For serious chocolate-tasting sessions, warm water is the best choice. It helps to clean the palate and warm the mouth, which will provide the perfect temperature at which to enjoy chocolate.

In contrast, there is no doubt that there is something childlike and comforting about chocolate served with a glass of cold milk. Pairings with alcohol, coffee or tea need more thought and are generally a more sophisticated affair. At Melt, we have collaborated with many fine wine companies, such as The Wine Society, Merry Widows Wine and the Australian company, Buller Wines, which has a stunning range of sweet, fortified wines. For some, we have created chocolates to match their wines; with others, we have incorporated their wines into our recipes.

The general rule of thumb is the sweeter the wine, the sweeter the chocolate should be, so milk chocolate can be a fairly good place to start. We have also found that our salty fresh chocolates, such as salted caramel (see page 149) and salted praline (see page 179), go well with sweet wine, creating wonderful excitement for the palate – salty, sweet, sticky and rich all combined in one wonderful hit.

My all-time favourite tipple with fresh chocolates is Domecq Venerable Pedro Ximenez, a 30-year-old sherry. The sticky, treacle-like texture is so incredibly indulgent with a single-origin dark chocolate truffle – I can't think of a better partner!

Coffee, a great bedfellow of chocolate, should also be considered. Many coffees have wonderful, naturally occurring chocolatey notes. One that I particularly enjoy is the Monmouth Coffee Company's organic Guatemalan coffee. At Melt we also like to use coffee from niche, small farms, such as those distributed by the Sea Island Coffee Company. Their Hawaiian coffee has the most sublime consistency and taste.

Being first and foremost a coffee fiend, I approached chocolate and tea as partners quite late in the day. At Melt we have had a great deal of success with delicious fresh chocolates infused with high-quality teas, such as jasmine pearls and Earl Grey, but to drink tea alongside chocolate you need to experiment a step further and see what combinations give you the most enjoyment.

I personally prefer stronger teas, such as Earl Grey, used to infuse chocolate to make ganache, while softer teas such as Oolong, or floral teas such as Miller Harris's Thé Pétales, work best while eating chocolate. Approaching specialist companies such as Orange Pekoe for tea is always rewarding, as they are very enthusiastic and are happy to suggest thoughtful pairings with chocolate.

21

...tasting, eating and cooking with chocolate...

...chocolate essentials...

...A NOTE ON THE RECIPES...

We recommend you invest in some digital weighing scales before starting to cook from this book. They are not expensive and they will really help you in your efforts. In recipes where precision is important, the liquid ingredients are measured by weight rather than volume, for which you will find digital scales much easier.

•••

There are many recipes in this book that call for tempered chocolate. The method for tempering can be found on pages 32–33. It is the one way to guarantee perfect chocolate, so it's important that you get it right. The larger the volume of chocolate tempered, the longer the temper will hold. Therefore, it's easier to temper more chocolate than is actually required. You'll notice that most of the recipes in this book that feature tempered chocolate require you to temper 500g. That will often be too much for what you need, but any unused chocolate can easily be cooled and stored for future use.

•••

A note for American readers

The quantities in this book are listed in metric measures but not in American cups, so you will need some kitchen scales. Working with chocolate requires precision and accuracy and cups cannot give you this. Below are the American terms for some of the ingredients and equipment used in this book.

baking parchment = parchment paper
baking sheet = cookie sheet
baking tin = baking pan
bicarbonate of soda = baking soda
cake tin = cake pan
candied peel = confited peel
caster sugar = superfine sugar
cling film = plastic wrap
dark chocolate = semisweet chocolate
demerara sugar = brown granulated sugar
double cream = heavy cream
flaked almonds = slivered almonds
ground almonds = almond flour
icing sugar = powdered sugar
liquid glucose = glucose syrup
loaf tin = loaf pan
marzipan = almond paste
palette knife = metal spatula
piping bag = pastry bag
piping nozzle = piping tip
plain flour = all-purpose flour
roasting tin = roasting pan
sea salt = coarse salt
self-raising flour = self-rising flour
sieve = strainer
sugar thermometer = candy thermometer
sultanas = golden raisins
Swiss roll tin = jelly roll pan
tart tin = tart pan
vanilla pod = vanilla bean

CHOCOLATE CARAMEL

MILK	170g	½ vei… Boil
CREAM	500g	
SALT	8g	
BICARB	3g	
SOY LECITHINE	16g	
BUTTER	400g	
VALRHONA COCOA PATE [illegible]	750g	
CASTOR SUGAR	850g	Boil
GLUCOSE	200g	145°c

[illegible]

Heat to 115°c

Add Cream Butter

Chocolate

...A FEW SPECIALIST ITEMS...

Making chocolates can sometimes be a tricky business. To make your life easier
(and your chocolates look and taste more delicious!), it is worth investing in a few specialist items.
You should be able to pick these bits of equipment up at good kitchen shops and numerous online
stores (see list of suppliers, pages 182–183).

Digital weighing scales

Measuring ingredients accurately is vital when making chocolates – and of course the scales can be used for other recipes too. Make sure you buy scales that measure in 1g increments.

Digital food thermometer

During the chocolate-making process it is sometimes necessary to check the temperature of melted chocolate – it needs to be spot on for these recipes, so a digital thermometer is essential.

Sugar thermometer

Very useful for making sugar solutions. Saves time and avoids any guesswork.

Disposable piping bags

Single-use bags that don't need washing up!

Dipping forks

Long-handled, flat forks that are available in various shapes to assist in coating chocolates. Although dipping forks are the best tool for the job, you can use ordinary kitchen forks too.

Acetate sheets

Finished chocolates are placed on these thin sheets to set. They peel off easily when the chocolates are ready. Acetate sheets can be washed and re-used.

Metal scraper or metal palette knife

Used to smooth, flatten and remove excess chocolate, especially from moulded chocolates.

Moulds

At Melt we use polycarbonate moulds, which are available from some kitchen shops and specialist suppliers (see pages 182–183). You can also use flexible silicone moulds. For a cheap and cheerful alternative to professional moulds, you could use flexible ice-cube trays to start with, then invest in good-quality chocolate moulds later.

...chocolate essentials...

...MELTING...

There are three basic methods of melting chocolate. Our favourite way is simply to put it in the oven at a very low temperature. This results in chocolate that is easy to handle and minimises the possibility of producing lumpy, unevenly melted chocolate. If you overheat the chocolate, or if it comes into contact with water or steam, then it may 'seize' – i.e. thicken and turn lumpy. If this happens, the chocolate is fine to use for baking cakes but can't be used for making chocolates or ganache.

In the oven

Chop the chocolate, put it in a heatproof bowl and place in a very low oven (about 50°C) for 10–15 minutes, until smooth and melted, stirring once or twice with a rubber spatula.

In the microwave

Chop the chocolate and place it in a heatproof bowl. Heat it in 15-second bursts at medium power, stirring it with a rubber spatula between each heating, until it is smooth and melted.

Over simmering water

Chop the chocolate and place it in a heatproof bowl. Put the bowl over a pan of gently simmering water, making sure that the water doesn't touch the base of the bowl, and stir occasionally with a rubber spatula until the chocolate is smooth and melted.

...melt...

...TEMPERING...

There is one way to guarantee gorgeous, glossy chocolate – temper it! Well-tempered chocolate has a lovely shine, a characteristic chocolate 'snap' and a deliciously smooth mouth-feel.

So what is tempering? It is simply the process of melting chocolate, cooling it down and then heating it up again. This stabilises the fat crystals in the cocoa butter so the chocolate takes on an attractive shiny appearance. The white streaks that sometimes appear in chocolate after it has been stored at the wrong temperature, known as bloom, will not develop in tempered chocolate.

The larger the volume of chocolate tempered, the longer the temper will hold. So it is best to temper a minimum of 500g at a time. The unused chocolate can be cooled and stored in an airtight container, away from direct light, at 18°C (room temperature) for up to 3 months. Be sure to temper it again before using.

...HOW TO TEMPER CHOCOLATE...

1

Melt the chocolate

Finely chop 500g dark, milk or white chocolate. It doesn't matter exactly what cocoa solids percentage it is, but be sure to stick to 64–70 per cent for dark chocolate, 36–40 per cent for milk chocolate and 30–35 per cent for white.

Put 375g of the chopped chocolate in a heatproof bowl and place in the microwave. Heat it in 30-second bursts at medium power, opening the microwave door and stirring the chocolate with a rubber spatula between each heating, until it has reached the temperature indicated on the chart below (check it with a digital thermometer). Using a microwave is the quickest method. If you wish to melt the chocolate in the oven, simply follow the instructions on page 28.

2

Seed the chocolate

Add the remaining 125g finely chopped chocolate to the melted chocolate a little at a time – this process is known as seeding. Slowly stir after each addition of chopped chocolate until it has melted, and use a digital thermometer to check the temperature of the liquid chocolate until it has reached the temperature indicated on the chart below. You may not need all of the remaining cold chocolate to bring the chocolate to the correct temperature. If the melted chocolate has reached the desired temperature and still contains some lumps of solid chocolate, use an electric hand blender to smooth it out.

Temperatures for tempering chocolate

Type of chocolate	Melting	Seeding	Reheating
Dark chocolate	53–55°C	28–29°C	31–32°C
Milk chocolate	45–48°C	27–28°C	30°C
White chocolate	45–48°C	26–27°C	29°C

...melt...

3

Reheat the chocolate

This is the tricky part – the chocolate needs to be heated by just 2–4°C. Place the bowl in a microwave and heat it at medium power for just a few seconds. Check the temperature using a digital thermometer, following the chart below. Stir well to finish the tempering process.

4

Test the chocolate

To test that the chocolate has been tempered correctly, drizzle a small amount on to a palette knife or a piece of baking parchment. It should set hard in 5 minutes and be shiny and glossy. Check the chocolate is ready by touching it: if only the top layer has set, the cocoa butter underneath has separated and the chocolate is not tempered. If this is the case, then the whole process needs to be repeated.

Use the tempered chocolate immediately, so it is at the correct temperature. If it starts to cool and thicken slightly while you are using it, you can microwave it for a few seconds to keep the temperature constant. If it goes completely out of temper, however, you will have to repeat the entire tempering process.

33

...FABULOUS GANACHE...

Basic ganache, a blend of chocolate and cream (or sometimes other liquids, such as tea or fruit purée), is very easy to make. Left to set, it forms the foundation of many of the chocolates in this book but it can also be served warm as a simple chocolate sauce. You can flavour it by either infusing the cream or decorating the finished chocolates. Once you have mastered the basic ganache recipe, start to experiment and build up a repertoire.

...melt...

Play around with small quantities: 100ml of cream and 100g of your chosen chocolate. This will enable you to create a flavour bank and decide which of your recipes work, which flavours marry well and how long you like to infuse your cream with flavours to get the perfect strength. We like the feminine qualities of flowers, such as a couple of heads of fresh lavender, or the green, earthy freshness of herbs – try a large pinch of dried tarragon, for example.

...chocolate essentials...

3 ways to eat ganache...

Straight away
As soon as the ganache is ready, pour it over vanilla ice cream. In the summer you can add a seasonal element by serving it with fresh raspberries, strawberries, blackberries or gooseberry purée – whatever is in abundance. For a more exotic taste, scoop out the pulp of a passionfruit and add to the ice cream and sauce.

Once set
After 3 hours or so, use the ganache as a filling for Chocolate Macaroons (see page 164), Babies' Kisses (page 162) or butterfly fairy cakes, or as a cake topping or filling.

Next day
The ganache will be firm, like cold butter, and can be cut into cubes or rectangles or scooped, like you would a melon. Roll or dust the ganache (see page 43) to create a 'finish' and to bring in more flavours. Finely ground pistachio looks pretty, crushed pink peppercorns will add a lot of heat, or simply dust with cocoa power or icing sugar. Eat within 2–3 days.

24-hour ganache

24-hour ganache is basic ganache with the addition of fresh fruit as a flavouring (see pages 38–42). You need only about 50g to add a hint of fruitiness. The ganache will be bursting with freshness and flavour, but must be used within 24 hours.

...CHOCOLATE GANACHE...

This basic ganache is great for making classic truffles and is also a delicious and easy sauce for vanilla ice cream – so why not double the quantities and get a dessert out of it the night before? When making ganache, the important thing to remember is that you are actually making an emulsion of ingredients, and the finished result should have a shiny, creamy texture – similar to mayonnaise.

227ml carton of double cream
200g dark chocolate (60 per cent cocoa solids), finely chopped

Pour the cream into a small pan and place it over a medium heat. When it is just starting to bubble at the edges, remove the pan from the heat and add the chocolate pieces. Using a wooden spoon, gently stir from the centre to emulsify the mixture. You will end up with a rich, glossy sauce. If you want to serve it with ice cream, then it is ready to serve now.

Chocolate truffles

To make simple chocolate truffles, pour the ganache into a plastic box lined with baking parchment. Allow to cool and then leave in the fridge overnight.

Lift the ganache out of the box with the parchment paper and peel away the paper. Cut the ganache into rough squares. Sift some good-quality unsweetened cocoa powder on to a plate. Using a fork, gently turn the ganache squares over in the cocoa powder until completely coated.

Store in a cool place, but not the fridge, which would spoil the texture. Eat within 4 days.

...LAVENDER AND ORANGE BLOSSOM GANACHE...

We absolutely love this quirky recipe – it is so eccentric. The taste is soft and feminine and the crushed, crystallised violets are reminiscent of parma violets. It is particularly good with Babies' Kisses (page 162). The flavour has been introduced by infusing the cream. Bear in mind that oils from flowers and herbs get stronger over time.

100ml double cream
2 heads of fresh lavender
 (or 1 teaspoon dried lavender)
100g white chocolate, finely chopped
1 teaspoon orange flower water
1 teaspoon finely ground crystallised
 violets

Pour the cream into a small pan and heat until small bubbles appear at the edges. Remove the pan from the heat. Take the buds off the lavender heads and add to the cream. Poke and prod the lavender to release its oils and then set aside for 20 minutes or so.

Strain the cream through a sieve into a clean pan. Heat until small bubbles start to appear at the edges. Take off the heat and add the chopped chocolate and the orange flower water. Stir gently with a wooden spoon to emulsify the mixture and give a smooth and glossy ganache. Pour into a rectangular dish, about 12 x 20cm, lined with baking parchment. Scatter the violets on top and leave to set. Using a teaspoon, shape into small, bite-sized balls.

...RASPBERRY AND MILK CHOCOLATE GANACHE...

This ganache is very evocative of long, hot summer nights.
It's particularly good drizzled over or rippled through vanilla ice cream.

100ml double cream
100g milk chocolate (at least 35 per
    cent cocoa solids), finely chopped
50g fresh raspberries

Pour the cream into a small pan and heat until little bubbles appear at the edges. Take off the heat and immediately add the chopped chocolate. Using a wooden spoon, stir gently from the centre to emulsify the mixture and give a smooth, glossy sauce.

Add the raspberries to the chocolate. Poke, prod and break up the raspberries with a wooden spoon, then either drizzle the warm ganache over cakes or ice cream or leave it to set and then make into truffles (see opposite).

Variations

• Substitute ripe blackberries for the raspberries.
• Scoop passionfruit flesh out of the shell and use instead of raspberries.

...chocolate essentials...

stir stir stir stir stir stir stir stir

...FRUIT PURÉES...

Many of the chocolates in this book are filled with ganache made with fruit purées rather than cream. You can buy excellent ready-made ones (see pages 182–183 for suppliers) or make your own, as described below. Remember that if you are making raspberry, blackcurrant or passionfruit purée, you will need roughly double the weight of fresh fruit to produce the amount of purée stated in the recipe, because the seeds will be sieved out.

Raspberry or blackcurrant

Whiz fresh or thawed frozen raspberries or blackcurrants in a food processor or blender, then push through a sieve to remove the seeds. If you are making a very small amount of purée, you can simply crush the fruit with a fork and then sieve them.

Banana

Peel a ripe banana and mash it with a fork, then push through a sieve.

Lychee

Drain canned lychees thoroughly, whiz them to a purée in a food processor or blender and then push through a sieve.

Mango

Canned mango purée is available from most Indian food stores. Alternatively, peel and stone a ripe mango, then purée in a food processor or blender and push through a sieve.

Passionfruit

Cut ripe, wrinkled passionfruit in half and scoop out the contents. Push through a sieve to remove the seeds.

Rhubarb

Cut 200g rhubarb into slices 1cm thick. Put in a pan with 20g caster sugar and a couple of tablespoons of water. Cover and cook gently for 15 minutes or until completely soft. Push through a sieve and leave to cool.

42

...FILLING, SEALING, ROLLING, DIPPING, DUSTING...

Filling

When you make chocolates with a soft ganache, you need to pipe the ganache into little chocolate shells or cups to set (available from specialist suppliers, see pages 182–183). We call these bonbons, or cups, rather than truffles, which usually describes a piped or more free-form chocolate shape.

Sealing

After you have put your filling in chocolate shells or cups, it needs to be sealed with a little tempered chocolate to secure the filling, prevent air pockets and create a perfect round. Put some tempered chocolate in a disposable plastic piping bag and snip off the tip. Hold the piping bag just above the filling of the chocolate and squeeze until the hole is completely sealed and the chocolate is nicely rounded off. Leave to set and then roll in tempered chocolate as described below.

Rolling

Chocolate shells look much more attractive if you roll them in chocolate after sealing. Pick up a chocolate in one hand, scoop up some tempered chocolate in the other and roll the chocolate in your chocolatey palm. Try to work fast, otherwise the tempered chocolate will become too warm in your hand. Place on a sheet of baking parchment to set, or dust the chocolate (see opposite).

Dipping

Dipping is a way of coating chocolate cylinders, rectangles and square cups to give a smart, professional finish. Drop your chocolate into a bowl of tempered chocolate and push it gently under the surface so it is completely coated. Carefully scoop it out on a dipping fork and tap the fork a few times against the side of the bowl so any excess chocolate runs off. Slide the bottom of the fork over the edge of the bowl to remove the excess chocolate, then place the chocolate on a piece of baking parchment and slide the fork out from underneath. Wipe the dipping fork clean before you dip the next chocolate. You can then finish the chocolate in one of the following ways: (1) Garnish with crushed nuts, candied fruit, gold leaf, sea salt, or according to the instructions in the recipe; (2) Place a patterned transfer sheet on top and leave at room temperature for at least 6 hours or overnight. Carefully peel off the transfer; (3) Sift with cocoa powder or dust as per the instructions below.

Dusting

After rolling or dipping your chocolate, if you want a dusted finish, immediately drop it into a bowl of sifted cocoa powder or icing sugar, or crushed dacquoise (see page 115) and gently shake the bowl to coat the chocolate. Remove from the bowl and dust off the excess with your hands, then place the chocolate on a sheet of baking parchment.

...chocolate essentials...

Filling chocolate shells

Sealing

Rolling

Dusting

44

Dipping

Applying a transfer sheet

Sifting with cocoa powder

Garnishing

...chocolate essentials...

...CHOCOLATE HEARTS...

This idea was born at Louise's kitchen table and has been one of Melt's signature chocolates ever since. Customers write a love note on a piece of paper and we tie a ribbon round it like a scroll and then enclose it inside the two halves of a chocolate heart – to be discovered on opening. We have seen the sweetest messages in the past and men are definitely more romantic with their scribblings. You can try this at home or simply make the chocolate hearts for a lovely Valentine's Day present. You will need four 8cm-high heart moulds.

Makes 2

1 quantity of tempered milk chocolate
   (see pages 32–33)
1 teaspoon ground mixed spice
1 teaspoon pink peppercorns

Polish four 8cm-high heart moulds with cotton wool (this makes the chocolate shiny). Mix the tempered milk chocolate with the mixed spice.

With a ladle, pour enough chocolate into the moulds to coat them generously. Tap the side of the moulds to get rid of any air bubbles, then turn them upside down over the bowl of chocolate and tap again. Turn the moulds the right way up and scrape off any excess chocolate with a metal scraper. Leave in the fridge for a few minutes until the chocolate is half set – it should still feel soft but not sticky.

Repeat the whole process with the remaining chocolate. Leave until half set, then sprinkle with the pink peppercorns. Leave in the fridge to set completely.

Turn the hearts out of the moulds. Put a frying pan with a flat base over a medium heat and leave until it is hot – you should still be able to touch it, but only just. Briefly press each heart on the surface of the pan until the chocolate softens on the edges. You can quickly put a message inside one of the hearts now, if you like. Press 2 hearts together until they stick – this should take about 5 minutes. Store the hearts in an airtight container at room temperature.

... melt ...

...RASPBERRY HEARTS...

This award-winning chocolate needs a reasonable amount of patience and skill.
There are a number of elements to making up the finished chocolate, so it is not one to attempt
in a rush. It offers a good opportunity to try moulding, filling and finishing. The ganache you make
is a little more than you actually need, but it is not practical to make a smaller amount.
Spread the leftover ganache on some brioche as a delicious treat. You will need 48 heart moulds,
2.5cm high. See the step-by-step pictures on pages 50–51.

Makes 48

1 quantity of tempered dark chocolate
(see pages 32–33)
85g dark chocolate (66 per cent cocoa
solids), finely chopped
85g milk chocolate (40 per cent cocoa
solids), finely chopped
125g double or whipping cream
125g raspberry purée (see page 42)
50g caster sugar
35g liquid glucose
10g unsalted butter

Use cotton wool to polish 48 heart moulds, 2.5cm high (this makes the chocolate shiny). With a ladle, pour the tempered chocolate into the moulds.

Tap the side of the moulds to get rid of any air bubbles, then turn them upside-down over the bowl of chocolate and tap again. Turn the moulds the right way up and scrape off any excess chocolate with a metal scraper. Leave in the fridge until the chocolate is set.

To make the ganache, put the finely chopped dark and milk chocolate in a bowl. Put the cream and raspberry purée in a small pan and place over a medium heat. Bring to boiling point, then remove from the heat. Put the sugar and glucose in a separate pan over a high heat and cook until it turns golden. Remove from the heat and pour in the cream mixture a little at a time, stirring until well combined. Pass through a fine sieve on to the chopped chocolate and stir gently from the centre to emulsify. Leave until the temperature measures no higher than 45°C on a digital thermometer, then add the butter and stir until combined. Set aside to cool to body temperature.

Transfer the cooled ganache to a disposable piping bag, snip off the tip of the bag and pipe the mixture into the chocolate-coated moulds, filling them to 2mm from the top. Leave in a cool place, but not the fridge, for at least 6 hours or overnight, until the ganache is completely set.

Re-temper the chocolate and ladle it over the top to coat the hearts, then cover them with a sheet of acetate and run a metal scraper over the top to seal the chocolates. Leave in the fridge, still covered with the acetate, for about 10 minutes, until set. Peel off the acetate and turn the moulds upside down to remove the hearts.

Place the hearts in an airtight box and store at room temperature for up to 2 weeks.

Polishing the moulds

Turning the moulds upside-down after filling

Scraping off the excess chocolate

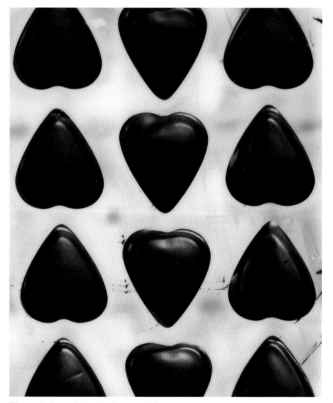

The set chocolates in the mould

... melt ...

Piping the ganache into the hearts

Sealing the chocolates

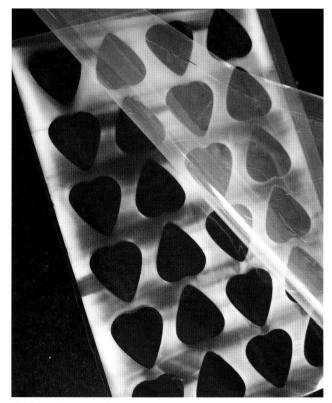

Peeling off the acetate

The finished hearts turned out of the moulds

...chocolate essentials...

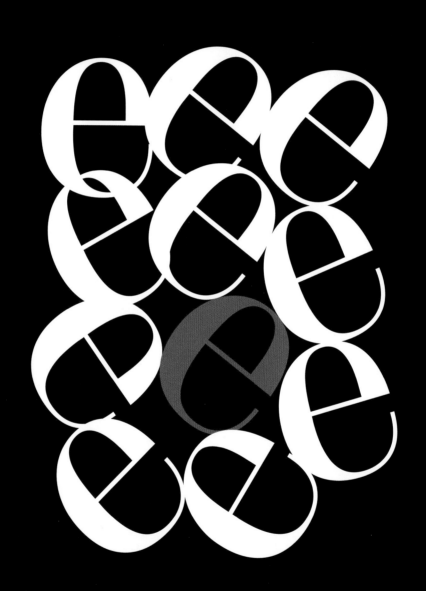

...EASTER EGGS...

Because it is our business, we invariably have chocolate within arm's reach many days of the year, but the only time we feel it is really appropriate to gorge on this wonderful food is at Easter. Starting first thing in the morning and just not stopping. It's the childish lack of control and the overwhelming abundance of sweetness at Easter that are so appealing. For Louise, it's got to be an egg – just a plain, simple chocolate egg. You will need ten 6cm-high egg moulds to make these. You can serve the eggs in egg cups, if you like, which is how we package them at Melt.

Makes 10 x 20g eggs

1 quantity of tempered milk chocolate or dark chocolate (see pages 32–33)

Polish ten 6cm-high egg moulds with cotton wool (this makes the chocolate shiny). With a ladle, pour about 300g of the tempered chocolate into the moulds.

Tap the side of the moulds to get rid of any air bubbles, then turn them upside-down over the bowl of chocolate and tap again. Turn the moulds the right way up and scrape off excess chocolate with a metal scraper. Leave in the fridge for a few minutes until the chocolate is half set – it should still feel soft but not sticky.

Repeat the whole process with more chocolate – you will end up using about 200g chocolate on the eggs in total. Leave in the fridge to set completely.

Turn the eggs out of the moulds. Put a frying pan with a flat base over a medium heat and leave until it is hot – you should still be able to touch it, but only just. Briefly press each egg half on the surface of the pan until the chocolate softens on the edges. Press 2 halves together until they stick – this should take about 5 minutes. Place the eggs in an airtight container and store at room temperature.

...spices
and
herbs...

...CHILLI AND PINK PEPPERCORN HOT CHOCOLATE...

Chocolate beans were first used as a beverage rather than a food. There is much evidence that the drink was actually given for medicinal purposes by the Aztecs, with *chacha* (a type of medicinal chocolate) comprising chocolate combined with honey, peppers and even tobacco juice. Chilli, native to the Americas, is one of the additional ingredients in this warming, fortifying drink. The strength of the chilli should be enough to make you nervous, but not enough to mask the chocolate.

Serves 2

300ml full-fat milk
120ml double cream
2 dried chillies
5 pink peppercorns
160g dark chocolate (at least 60 per cent cocoa solids), chopped
2 strips of lime zest
$\frac{1}{2}$ teaspoon good-quality vanilla extract
$\frac{1}{2}$ teaspoon maple syrup

Pour the milk and cream into a small pan. Break the dried chillies in half, shake out and discard the seeds, then add the chillies to the milk and cream, along with the pink peppercorns. Place over a medium heat until bubbles appear around the rim. Set aside for 5–10 minutes to let the flavours infuse.

Place the chopped chocolate in a heatproof jug. Reheat the milk mixture until it is just about to boil, then pour it through a sieve on to the chocolate. Stir until melted. Add the lime zest, vanilla extract and maple syrup and stir well. If the chocolate hasn't quite melted, reheat the mixture gently. Serve in warmed mugs. Watch out for the extra heat at the bottom of the cup!

No wonder the Spanish conquistador, Hernan Cortés, said,
'A cup of this precious drink permits a man to walk for a whole day without food.'

...GINGER MILK BONBONS...

Ginger goes incredibly well with milk chocolate. You can also dip crystallised chunks into dark chocolate for a wonderful finale after dinner. We prefer to use organic crystallised ginger, as it tends to have less sweetness and a much more fiery heat – perfect for jaded palates. Ginger tea is very pleasant to drink while eating chocolate. To make it, simply put 3–4 shavings of fresh root ginger into a cup, add boiling water and leave it to steep for 3 minutes, then enjoy!

Makes 50

150g double cream
20g full-fat milk
20g liquid glucose
25g fresh ginger, grated
185g milk chocolate (35–40 per cent cocoa solids), finely chopped
20g unsalted butter, cut into small cubes
50 milk chocolate cups (see page 43)
tempered milk chocolate, for sealing (see pages 32–33)
50 pieces of freeze-dried passionfruit, to decorate (optional)

Place the double cream, milk and glucose in a small pan, bring to the boil, then remove from the heat. Add the grated ginger and set aside to infuse for 3 minutes.

Put the chopped chocolate in a bowl. Strain the infused cream through a fine sieve to remove the ginger, return it to the pan and bring to the boil again. Pour it over the chocolate and stir gently from the middle to emulsify.

Check on a digital thermometer that the temperature is no higher than 45°C, then stir in the butter until it is well combined. Leave the mixture to cool to body temperature. Cut the tip off a disposable piping bag to leave a 3mm hole, then fill the bag with the mixture and pipe it into the chocolate cups. Set the chocolates aside in a cool place for at least 6 hours or overnight for the filling to set.

Seal the chocolates with the tempered milk chocolate (see page 43) and place a piece of passionfruit on top of each one to decorate, if you have it.

...CHILLI CUBES...

It was huge demand from our customers that led to the creation of our chilli chocolate, and one of our youngest chocolatiers, Darren Cafferty, was eager to devise a recipe. Although it may appear an unusual or modern marriage of flavours, it is actually one of the original pairings for chocolate, first tried by the Mayas and Aztecs from 600–1200AD in South America. Chilli was added for heat, spice and to mask bitterness. At Melt, the chilli cube fluctuates according to the latest feedback. Some say too hot... some say not hot enough! There is a delicious feeling of anticipation as you wait for the heat to come through.

Makes 72

250g double cream
20g liquid glucose
35g full-fat milk
2–3g dried chilli flakes, plus a few to decorate
200g dark chocolate (70 per cent cocoa solids), finely chopped
20g unsalted butter, cut into small cubes
tempered dark chocolate, for dipping (see pages 32–33)

Line a 20 x 30 baking tin with cling film.

Put the cream, glucose and milk in a small pan and bring to the boil. Remove from the heat and add the chilli. Leave to infuse for 10–20 minutes, depending on the strength of the chilli (taste it to check).

Put the chopped chocolate in a bowl and strain the hot cream on to it through a fine sieve. Stir gently from the middle to emulsify. Check on a digital thermometer that the temperature is no higher than 45°C, then stir in the cubed butter until melted and thoroughly combined.

Pour the mixture into a 20 x 30cm baking tin lined with cling film. Leave in a cool place for at least 6 hours or overnight, until set.

Cut the chocolate into squares, rectangles – or whatever shape you like – with a large, sharp knife. Dip the pieces in the tempered chocolate (see page 43) and sprinkle a few chilli flakes on top of each one.

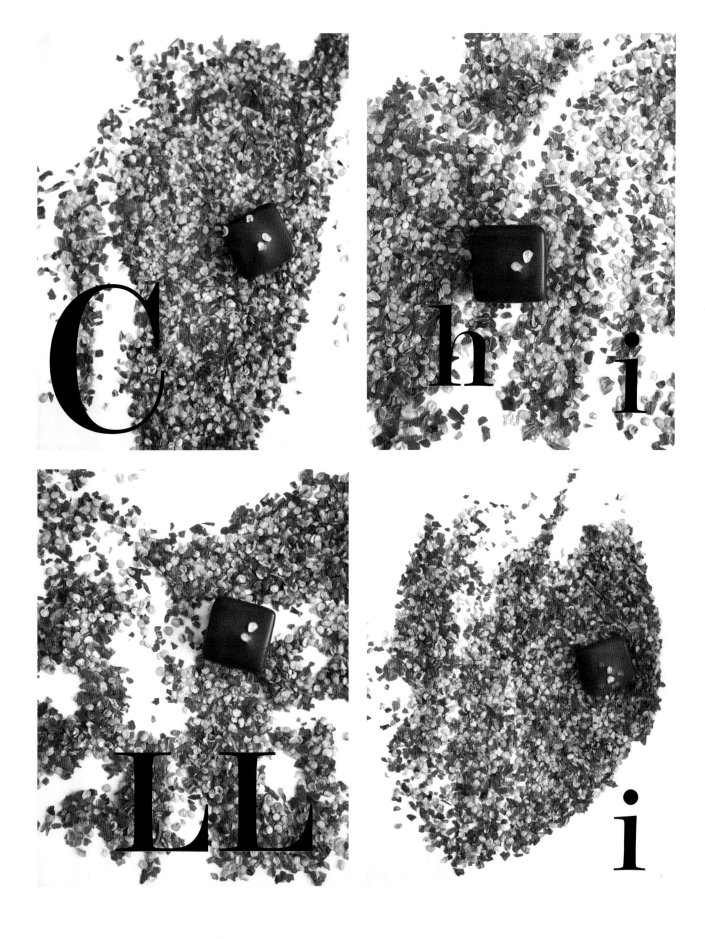

...STAR ANISE-SCENTED WHITE CHOCOLATE MOUSSE WITH FIG AND PRUNE COMPOTE...

This white chocolate mousse on its own has a comforting, childlike taste.
The fig and prune compote takes it to a more sophisticated level.
The compote can be made in advance and reheated with a little extra water.

Serves 6

475ml double cream
2 star anise
2 teaspoons agar flakes
200g white chocolate, chopped

For the fig and prune compote
3 ripe fresh figs, roughly chopped
3 soft prunes, roughly chopped
3 tablespoons kirsch
5 tablespoons water
a tiny sprig of thyme

Heat half the double cream in a small pan with the star anise until small bubbles appear, then leave to cool. Sprinkle the agar flakes on to the cream and return the pan to the heat. When small bubbles appear, stir every couple of minutes until the flakes have dissolved. Remove from the heat and leave to cool again. Take out the star anise and discard.

Meanwhile, place the chopped white chocolate in a heatproof bowl and put in a cool oven (about 50°C) for 15 minutes or until melted, stirring gently once or twice. Pour the cream mixture over the melted chocolate and stir well to combine.

Whisk the remaining cream in a large bowl until just getting stiff. Add the cream and chocolate mixture and give another whisk until thick and fluffy. Spoon into 6 individual serving bowls or glasses. You can chill the mousse if you like, which will make the texture firmer but equally delicious.

For the compote, place all the ingredients, in a small pan, bring to a simmer and cook gently for 25–30 minutes, until the fruit is very soft and the liquid has reduced to a syrup. During cooking, poke the figs a bit with a wooden spoon so the seeds get released into the syrup, which looks pretty. If the liquid boils away before the fruit is soft, just add a little more water.

To serve, spoon the warm compote over the fluffy white mousse.

...SPICE CUPS...

The taste of these chocolates always reminds us of the busy Christmas season.
The warmth of the spices intermingling with the silky, smooth milk chocolate is so soothing.
Spices like nutmeg, cardamon and cinnamon go particularly well with creamy milk chocolate
ganaches and recipes that call for milk chocolate.

Makes 50

220g milk chocolate (35 per cent cocoa
   solids), finely chopped
200g double cream
25g unsalted butter, cut into small
   cubes
a pinch of ground star anise
a pinch of ground cardamom
a pinch of ground mixed spice
10g Cognac
50 milk chocolate cups (see page 43)
tempered milk chocolate, for sealing
   (see pages 32–33)
50 small dice of candied orange peel, to
   decorate

Put the chopped milk chocolate in a
bowl. Put the cream into a small pan
and bring just to boiling point, then
remove from the heat and pour on to
the chocolate. Stir gently from the
middle to emulsify.

Check on a digital thermometer that the
temperature is no higher than 45°C,
then stir in the butter, spices and
Cognac until combined. When the
mixture has cooled to body
temperature, cut 3mm off the end of a
disposable piping bag, then fill the bag
with the mixture and pipe it into the
chocolate cups. Leave for at least 6
hours or overnight to allow them to set.

Seal the chocolate cups with the
tempered milk chocolate (see page 43).
Decorate each chocolate with a piece
of candied orange peel.

...spices and herbs...

...TONKA FEUILLETINE...

This is one of our most popular chocolates, the sweetness and texture being its winning characteristics. Tonka beans (see pages 182–183 for stockists) are also known as poor man's vanilla. They are highly perfumed and best used sparingly – grated into cream while making a ganache or used as decoration. Grate the tonka bean on a nutmeg grater for the best results. At Melt we make most things from scratch but, given the lack of baking facilities, we use ready-made feuilletine – a thin, biscuity wafer. An excellent substitute at home is good-quality waffle ice cream cones, crushed.

Makes 64

1 quantity of tempered dark chocolate (66 per cent cocoa solids) (see pages 32–33)
1 quantity of tempered milk chocolate (see pages 32–33)
310g praline paste
125g good-quality waffle ice cream cones, finely crushed
2 pinches of grated tonka bean, plus extra to decorate

Line a 20cm square baking tin with baking parchment.

Put 125g of the tempered dark chocolate, 50g of the tempered milk chocolate and the praline paste in a bowl and mix well (you won't need the remaining dark chocolate but if keeps well). Stir in the crushed ice cream cones and grated tonka.

Pour the chocolate mixture into the prepared tin. Tap it on the work surface to smooth the top and then leave in a cool place for at least 6 hours or overnight to set.

Invert the tray to remove the chocolate mixture, then peel off the parchment and cut the chocolate into 2.5cm squares. Dip the squares into the remaining tempered milk chocolate (see page 43). Sprinkle a little grated tonka over, then leave to set.

...CHILLI BARS...

For this recipe, cocoa butter is infused with dried chilli – we use wonderful organic bird's eye chilli flakes from Steenbergs which are excellent quality.
Infusing for a few hours will give these bars a wonderfully warming taste.
You will need ten 50g bar moulds.

Makes 10 x 50g bars

50g cocoa butter
1 dried chilli, roughly crushed
1 quantity of tempered dark chocolate
(see pages 32–33)

Put the cocoa butter in a small pan and heat gently until it melts. Add the chilli and remove from the heat. Cover the pan with a lid and set aside to infuse for 3 hours.

Remove the crushed chilli from the butter and weigh out 20g of the infused butter. Combine the infused butter with the tempered chocolate.

Polish ten 50g bar moulds with cotton wool (this makes the bars shiny). Cut the tip off a disposable piping bag to leave an 8mm hole. Pour the chocolate into the piping bag and pipe into the prepared moulds to the top. Leave in the fridge to set completely.

Turn the bars out of the moulds and wrap them in baking parchment.

...CARDAMOM, STRAWBERRY AND RASPBERRY ON DARK CHOCOLATE...

Mixing natural dried strawberry and raspberry together looks very pretty against the dark chocolate, one being dark pink, the other more red. The cardamom adds a lovely exotic element. Once the basic slab has been mastered, myriad fruits, nuts and spices can be used – the combinations are limitless.

1 quantity of tempered dark chocolate
(see pages 32–33)
10g freeze-dried strawberries
10g freeze-dried raspberries
a pinch of ground cardamom

Mix the strawberries, raspberries and cardamom together in a small bowl.

Put a 40 x 30cm sheet of acetate on a chopping board. Spread 300g of the chocolate on to the acetate with a palette knife in a layer 2mm thick (you won't need the remaining tempered chocolate but it stores well). Sprinkle the dried ingredients on to the chocolate while it is still liquid. Leave to set.

Break the chocolate into pieces to serve.

...ROSEMARY AND CITRUS ON WHITE CHOCOLATE...

This recipe was designed for a company wanting a light, summery chocolate for their clients visiting the Chelsea Flower Show. The sweet white chocolate acts as the perfect base for the fresh, fruity bursts of natural orange zest and grapefruit and the contrasting grassy rosemary. Cocoa nibs are crushed, roasted cocoa beans, which are ground to make chocolate. They can also be eaten before grinding. They have a hard, gritty texture and an earthy taste.

grated zest of 1 orange
20 drops of grapefruit essential oil
1 quantity of tempered white chocolate
   (see pages 32–33)
20g cocoa nibs
10g dried rosemary

Spread the orange zest out on a baking tray and leave it in a warm place, such as an airing cupboard or a warm room, for a day to dry; it should be dry enough to crumble to a powder between your fingers.

Add the grapefruit oil to the tempered white chocolate. Put a 40 x 30cm sheet of acetate on a board. Spread 300g of the chocolate on to the acetate in a layer 3mm thick, using a palette knife. Sprinkle with the cocoa nibs, rosemary and a pinch of the powdered orange zest and leave to set. Break into shards to serve.

...DARK CHOCOLATE DISCS WITH DRIED RASPBERRIES...

Fruits such as raspberry have a special affinity with chocolate. 'Red fruits' is a term used to describe a particular chocolate flavour note and is especially characteristic of chocolate from Madagascar. Buy naturally dried fruits (see pages 182–183 for Suppliers), as you want tartness, not sweetness, to dovetail with the chocolate.

Makes 30

10g freeze-dried raspberries, crumbled
    into pieces no bigger than 2mm
1 quantity of tempered dark chocolate
    (see pages 32–33)

Put a 40 x 30cm sheet of acetate on a chopping board. Snip the end off a disposable piping bag to leave a 7mm hole. Mix the freeze-dried raspberries with half the chocolate and pour the mixture into the piping bag (you won't need the rest of the chocolate here but it keeps well). Squeeze the chocolate on to the acetate in thin rounds about 3cm in diameter, leaving them very well spaced out. Carefully place a second acetate sheet on top of the chocolate, then cover with a chopping board and leave for about 10 minutes, until the chocolates are about 2mm thick.

Leave to set, allowing 6 hours before removing the acetate so the chocolate is beautifully shiny.

...JAPANESE SHICHIMI CHILLI SQUARES...

Shichimi togarashi is a Japanese spice mixture that dates back to the 17th century. It is made up of seven ingredients, namely coarsely ground red chilli pepper (the predominant spice), ground sansho, roasted orange peel, black sesame seeds, white sesame seeds, seaweed and ground ginger. It is often used to flavour soups, noodles and rice cakes and can be served as a simple table condiment. Here it gives a fiery kick to these dark chocolate squares.

Makes 50 squares

250g double cream
20g liquid glucose
15g full-fat milk
2 teaspoons Japanese shichimi chilli, plus a little more to garnish
10g orange zest
200g dark chocolate (70 per cent cocoa solids), finely chopped
20g unsalted butter, cut into small cubes
tempered dark chocolate, for dipping (see pages 32–33)

Pour the cream, glucose and milk into a saucepan. Add the chilli and orange zest and bring the mixture to the boil. Remove from the heat and leave to infuse for 10–20 minutes, depending on how much you want the chilli to flavour the cream (taste it to check).

Put the chopped chocolate in a bowl and strain the hot cream on to it through a fine sieve. Stir gently from the centre until it emulsifies. When the temperature measures no more than 45°C on a digital thermometer, stir in the butter until combined.

Line a 20cm square baking tin with cling film, pour in the mixture and leave in a cool place for at least 6 hours or overnight, until set.

Use a large, sharp knife to cut the chocolate into squares or rectangles. Dip in the tempered chocolate (see page 43) and sprinkle a little shichimi chilli on top of each square.

...MINT AND RASPBERRY WHITE CHOCOLATE BONBONS...

These are great chocolates – routinely pre-ordered by an antiques dealer on Portobello Road to keep him going on a busy Saturday! Although white chocolate has no cocoa solids and therefore isn't strictly speaking chocolate, its sweet, straightforward base creates the perfect backdrop for chocolates and desserts. In this case it adds a creamy sweetness to a fabulous burst of raspberry ganache and tingly mint.

Makes 50

90g white chocolate (30–35 per cent cocoa solids), finely chopped
135g raspberry purée (see page 42)
35g caster sugar
20g liquid glucose
35g unsalted butter, cut into small cubes
50 white chocolate shells (see page 43)
tempered white chocolate (see pages 32–33), for rolling
1 tablespoon crystallised mint leaves (see Suppliers, page 183), crushed

Place the chopped white chocolate in a bowl.

Put the raspberry purée, caster sugar and glucose in a small pan and bring to the boil, then remove from the heat. Pour on to the white chocolate and stir gently from the middle to emulsify. Check on a digital thermometer that the temperature is no higher than 45°C, then stir in the butter until combined. When the mixture has cooled to body temperature, pipe it into the chocolate shells. Set aside in a cool place for at least 6 hours or overnight for the filling to firm up.

Combine the tempered white chocolate with the crushed crystallised mint leaves. Seal and roll the chocolates using the white mint chocolate as described on page 43.

...nuts and seeds...

...CHOCOLATE GRANOLA...

This is the most glamorous granola – and makes a hedonistic start to the day scattered liberally on yogurt. It's perfect to give as a present in a pretty jar. Be inventive and use any mix of oats, nuts and even spices.

Ask children to design their own muesli base. Little hands can mix the dry ingredients, which is fun and tactile.

200g rolled oats
50g hazelnuts
50g unblanched almonds
50g desiccated coconut
50g sunflower seeds
6 Medjool dates, stoned and torn up
    into smaller pieces
200g runny honey
200g dark chocolate (at least 60 per
    cent cocoa solids)

Preheat the oven to 200°C/Gas Mark 6.

Put all the dry ingredients in a bowl and mix well. Add the honey and stir until evenly mixed. Place the mixture in a roasting tray and toast in the oven for about 15 minutes, until the nuts and oats are beginning to turn golden brown, stirring the mixture every 5 minutes to ensure even toasting. Remove from the oven and leave to cool.

Smash up the chocolate with a rolling pin on a wooden chopping board, or using a pestle and mortar, to create small nuggets. Add the chocolate to the granola and spoon into an airtight jar – I use a 1-litre Le Parfait jar. Eat straight, as a highly moreish snack, or scatter on Greek yogurt.

...POPCORN SLAB...

We designed this chocolate for a film premiere. It is a popular recipe with a youthful, fun taste. The arm you see modelling it belongs to our very talented, mild-mannered chocolatier, Michael Lowe.

530g tempered milk chocolate or tempered dark chocolate (see pages 32–33)

For the caramelised popcorn
1 tablespoon vegetable oil
30g popcorn kernels
50g caster sugar
5g unsalted butter

First, you need to 'pop' the corn. Put the oil into a large pan and set it over a medium heat. Add the kernels, cover with a lid and heat until they start to 'pop'. Shake the pan to ensure that all the corn pops. When it has finished popping, remove from the heat and tip the popcorn into a large bowl, taking out any kernels that haven't popped. Set aside.

Wipe the pan out with kitchen paper to remove any oil and set it back over a medium heat. Pour the sugar into the pan and stir until it begins to bubble and turns golden. Then add the butter and keep stirring until it has melted into the caramel. Remove the pan from the heat and then tip in the popped corn immediately. Mix well, ensuring that all of the popcorn is coated with the caramel. Leave to cool.

Place 70g of the caramelised popcorn in a bowl, add the tempered chocolate and mix together. Spread the mixture on to a sheet of baking parchment in a layer about 1cm thick (the same height as the popcorn). Place in the fridge and leave for 5 minutes or until set. Break the chocolate into rough chunks to serve.

81

...STRIP BAR...

Sesame seeds are a fairly modern addition to chocolate recipes and work very well. Caramelising the seeds first adds sweetness and flavour. These bars have a strip of caramelised sesame running through and we just had to call it the rather cheeky-sounding Strip Bar. You will need ten 50g bar moulds.

Makes 10 x 50g bars

1 quantity of tempered milk chocolate (see pages 32–33)

For the caramelised sesame seeds
20g caster sugar
30g water
35g sesame seeds

To caramelise the sesame seeds, place the sugar and water in a small pan and bring to the boil, stirring to dissolve the sugar. Add the sesame seeds all at once, then stir constantly over a medium heat until the water has evaporated and the seeds are a light brown colour, but not too sticky. Remove from the heat, tip them out on to a piece of baking parchment and leave to cool.

Polish ten 50g bar moulds with cotton wool (this makes the bars shiny). Cut the tip off a disposable piping bag to leave an 8mm hole. Pour half the tempered milk chocolate into the piping bag and pipe into the prepared moulds, filling them half full. Sprinkle on the caramelised sesame, then leave at room temperature till semi-set.

When the seeds are sticking to the chocolate, pipe in the rest of the tempered chocolate, filling the moulds to the top. Leave in the fridge to set completely.

Turn the bars out of the moulds and wrap them in baking parchment.

...WHITE BROWNIES WITH PECANS AND HAZELNUTS...

This recipe offers all the satisfaction and moreishness of regular chocolate brownies. They are deliciously moist and keep well. If there are by chance any left over, they taste even better the next day, as they become more dense. You can substitute different nuts, if you prefer.

Makes about 20

50g pecan nuts
50g hazelnuts
150g unblanched almonds
350g white chocolate
200g unsalted butter, diced
300g golden caster sugar
100g self-raising flour, sifted
4 organic eggs
icing sugar, for dusting

Preheat the oven to 180°C/Gas Mark 4. Line a 20 x 30cm baking tin with baking parchment.

Place the pecans and hazelnuts on a baking tray and toast them in the oven for 6–8 minutes, until just starting to brown. Set aside to cool. Reduce the oven temperature to 50°C.

Grind the almonds in a coffee grinder or food processor until fine but still retaining some texture.

Chop 250g of the white chocolate into chunks and place in a large heatproof bowl with the butter. Place in the oven for 10–15 minutes until melted, stirring gently once or twice. Remove from the oven. Increase the oven temperature to 160°C/Gas Mark 3.

Place the sugar, ground almonds, flour and eggs in a large bowl and mix well. Add the melted white chocolate and butter and stir until completely combined. Bash the pecans and hazelnuts into irregular-sized chunks and add to the mixture. Chop the remaining 100g of white chocolate into irregular-sized chunks and stir them in too.

Pour the mixture into the prepared tin and bake for 40–45 minutes, until golden brown. Leave to cool in the tin, then turn out and cut into squares or rectangles. Dust liberally with icing sugar to serve.

...CHOCOLATE POWER BARS...

Crammed with fruit, seeds and chocolate, these bars are powerful stuff and just the right thing to take on a long walk or camping trip. Louise's four children all got to the top of Ben Nevis with these as essential supplies and Ben was only four years old!

Makes 10–12

100g shredded dried coconut
50g raisins
50g pumpkin seeds
3 large Medjool dates, finely chopped
200g dark chocolate (around 70 per
    cent cocoa solids), finely chopped

Preheat the oven to 180°C/Gas Mark 4.

Put all the ingredients except the chocolate in a 23cm square baking tin. Roast in the oven for 5–10 minutes, turning the mixture regularly, until golden brown. Remove from the oven and set aside.

Put the chopped chocolate into a heatproof bowl and leave in a low oven (about 50°C) for about 15 minutes, until melted, stirring gently once or twice.

Tip all the roasted ingredients into the bowl of melted chocolate and mix well. Line the tin with baking parchment, return the mixture to the tin and press down to create an even layer. Score into rectangular bars with a knife, then leave in the fridge to set for 30 minutes or so.

Ease the bars out of the tin when set. Wrap in baking parchment for walks and family adventures!

...RICH CHOCOLATE ALMOND CAKE...

Luscious, moist and chocolatey, this is all one could ever want from a chocolate cake.
This page of the book is likely to become sticky and well thumbed!
For decoration, you could make stencils with pieces of card and place them on the cake.
Simply sift icing sugar over and then take the stencils off.

120g dark chocolate (at least 70 per cent cocoa solids), finely chopped
60g whole blanched almonds
120g unsalted butter, softened
120g golden caster sugar
3 organic eggs, separated
2–4 drops of almond extract
2 tablespoons strong black coffee
60g plain flour, sifted
a pinch of salt
icing sugar, for dusting (optional)

Put the dark chocolate into a heatproof bowl and leave in a low oven (about 50°C) for about 15 minutes, until melted, stirring gently once or twice. Increase the oven temperature to 150°C/Gas Mark 2.

Place the almonds on a baking tray and toast them in the oven for 5–10 minutes or until golden brown. Cool the nuts and then grind finely in a coffee grinder or food processor.

Increase the oven temperature to 180°C/Gas Mark 4. Grease a 23cm round cake tin with butter and dust with flour.

In a large mixing bowl, cream the butter and sugar together until pale and fluffy. Gradually add the egg yolks, beating constantly. Using a spatula, stir in the melted chocolate and the almond extract; the mixture should look glossy and appetising. Add the strong black coffee and gently fold the flour in.

Whisk the eggs whites briskly with the salt until they are stiff and voluminous, but not dry. Fold the almonds into the chocolate mixture, followed by the egg whites, a spoonful at time. Be gentle, so you don't knock out the air from the whites.

Turn the mixture into the prepared cake tin and bake for 25 minutes. The cake is done when the surface looks matt and a knife inserted in the centre comes out clean. Let it cool in the tin. The centre may sink a little, but this will not detract from its deliciousness.

...SESAME, TAHINI AND COCOA NIB MOUSSE...

This mousse is extremely quick and simple. It looks very pretty too, and the sesame seed and cocoa nib topping makes an interesting, crunchy texture in contrast to the rich, silky mousse. The earthy flavour of the tahini can be detected when the mousse is warm, but once cooled it is very subtle and just heightens the sesame element.

Serves 4

150ml double cream
100g dark chocolate (66 per cent cocoa solids), roughly chopped
2 tablespoons whole or light tahini
1 scant tablespoon golden syrup
1 organic egg yolk
30g sesame seeds
30g cocoa nibs

Place the cream in a small pan and heat until small bubbles start to show. Remove from the heat, add the chocolate and stir gently until the chocolate has melted. Stir in the tahini and golden syrup. You will have a thick, glossy mixture. Pour the mixture into a bowl, add the egg yolk and mix thoroughly.

Toast the sesame seeds in a frying pan over a low heat for a couple of minutes. Add the cocoa nibs and toast for 5 minutes longer, or until the sesame seeds are pale golden, but not browned.

Spoon the mousse into individual glasses or ramekins, scatter over the sesame and cocoa nib mixture and chill. It's best served within 2–3 hours, while it's still quite soft.

...STRIP BAR CUPCAKES...

This recipe takes cupcakes to a whole new level, and the different tastes and textures are really quite unusual. They were created by Marta Karcz, one of the Melt team, and she was inspired by the strip of caramelised sesame seeds that make up the Melt Strip Bar (see page 82). The tahini topping is divine and also works well on a large, plain chocolate cake, made using the cake mix below.

Makes 24

For the cakes
220g plain flour
60g cocoa powder
1 1/2 teaspoons baking powder
1 1/2 teaspoons bicarbonate of soda
1 teaspoon salt
425g caster sugar
2 large organic eggs
250ml full-fat milk
125ml vegetable oil (such as mild olive oil)
1 tablespoon vanilla extract
250ml boiling water
30g unsalted butter
2 tablespoons light tahini
300g digestive biscuits, crushed to crumbs
180g sesame seeds, half coarsely ground, the rest left whole
250g dark chocolate (70 per cent cocoa solids), coarsely grated

For the tahini and cream cheese icing
400g icing sugar
100g unsalted butter, at room temperature
200g cream cheese, from the fridge
4 tablespoons light tahini
40g dark chocolate (70 per cent cocoa solids), coarsely grated

Preheat the oven to 180°C/Gas Mark 4. Line 2 x 12-hole muffin tins with paper cases and set aside.

Sift the flour, cocoa powder, baking powder, bicarbonate of soda and salt into an electric mixer and add 400g of the sugar. Using the paddle attachment, mix the ingredients together on low speed.

In a large bowl, mix together the eggs, milk, oil and vanilla extract. Add to the flour mixture and beat on medium speed for 30 seconds. Scrape down the sides of the bowl and continue mixing on medium speed for 2 minutes. Add the boiling water and stir to combine.

Put the butter and tahini in a small pan and heat gently until melted. Place the biscuit crumbs, sesame seeds and the remaining caster sugar in a bowl, add the tahini mixture and stir until well combined. Place 1 tablespoon of the mixture in the bottom of each muffin case. Use the base of a small glass to pack the mixture in firmly. Reserve the remaining mixture for the topping.

Place 2 teaspoons of grated chocolate in each muffin case. Reserve the remaining chocolate for the topping. Bake for about 5 minutes, until the edges of the biscuit mixture are golden. Remove from the oven and fill each case three-quarters full with the cake batter. Sprinkle with the remaining chocolate and the digestive biscuit mixture, then return to the oven and bake for 18–20 minutes, until the tops are firm and a skewer inserted in the centre comes out clean. Transfer to a wire rack and let the cupcakes cool in the tins for 10 minutes. Remove from the tins and leave to cool completely.

To make the icing, beat the icing sugar and butter together with an electric mixer on medium speed until the mixture comes together. Add the cream cheese and tahini in one go and beat until completely incorporated, light and fluffy – but don't overbeat, otherwise it can turn too runny. Gently stir in the chocolate. Decorate the cooled cupcakes with the icing.

...COCOA CANAPÉS...

This recipe is so simple and really is one of the few sweet canapés that can work with champagne. Children will find the sifting fun to do – adults will like eating the canapés with an apéritif.

Serves 20–30

100g icing sugar
50g good-quality unsweetened cocoa
    powder
400g blanched almonds

Preheat the oven to 150°C/Gas Mark 2.

Sift the icing sugar and cocoa powder into a bowl and mix together (this creates the chicest purple-brown colour imaginable). Place the almonds in a separate bowl, add 4 tablespoons of cold water and stir just to moisten them.

Remove the almonds with a slotted spoon and place them in the cocoa powder mixture. Roll them around to coat thoroughly, then remove in batches with the slotted spoon and shake, rattle and roll them around the spoon, getting rid of excess powder, but leaving a good coating.

Place the nuts in an even layer in an ovenproof dish about 20 x 30cm. Cook in the oven for 15 minutes. Watch the nuts like a hawk and turn them regularly. You are looking for darker patches, but not burnt. Set aside to cool.

Serve the nuts in bowls, with champagne or chilled sweet wine.

...ROCHERS...

This is an old-fashioned type of chocolate made using roasted almond batons
bound together with chocolate to create a mini hedgehog shape.
We also include a little candied orange peel to add a lovely citrus note.

Makes 30

50g caster sugar
50g water
1 vanilla pod, halved lengthwise and
    seeds scraped out
150g blanched almonds, cut into small,
    slim batons
20g icing sugar
1 quantity of tempered dark chocolate
    (see pages 32–33)
5g cocoa butter, melted
15g candied orange peel, finely
    chopped

Preheat the oven to 120°C/Gas
Mark ½.

First make a vanilla syrup. Place the
caster sugar, water, vanilla pod and
seeds in a small pan and bring to the
boil, stirring to dissolve the sugar.
Simmer for 3 minutes, then remove
from the heat. This makes more syrup
than you will need but it isn't really
practical to make a smaller amount.

Place the almonds in a bowl. Pour over
15g of the vanilla syrup and stir well to
coat the almonds. Sprinkle the icing
sugar over the almonds to coat.
Spread the sugar-coated almonds
out on a baking tray lined with baking
parchment. Bake in the oven for
5 minutes, to dry the nuts out. Remove
from the oven and set aside to cool.

Place 100g of the dark chocolate in a
bowl (you won't need the remaining
chocolate for this but it keeps well).
Add the melted cocoa butter and mix
well. Add the roasted almonds and
candied orange peel and stir well until
thoroughly combined. Scoop
teaspoonfuls of the mixture on to a
baking tray lined with baking parchment
and leave the chocolates to set in a
cool place.

...LA FROMAGERIE
ALMOND BAR...

La Fromagerie in London is one of our all-time favourite shops. Patricia Michelson and Sarah Bilney were very specific about the almonds they wanted us to use for their milk chocolate almond bar – the superior Marcona almonds from south-eastern Spain, which have a lovely, milky sweetness to them. You will need ten 50g bar moulds.

Makes 10 x 50g bars

100g whole blanched Marcona
  almonds (approximately 10 per bar)
1 quantity of tempered milk chocolate
  (see pages 32–33)

Preheat the oven to 120°C/Gas Mark $^1/_2$.

Place the almonds on a baking tray and roast them in the oven for about 10 minutes, until they are a light brown colour. Remove from the oven and set aside to cool.

Polish ten 50g bar moulds with cotton wool (this makes the bars shiny). Cut the tip off a disposable piping bag to leave a 5mm hole. Pour the tempered milk chocolate into the piping bag and pipe into the prepared moulds, filling them almost to the top.

Divide the roasted almonds equally among the moulds. Leave in the fridge to set completely, then turn out of the moulds and wrap in baking parchment.

...CARAMELISED NUTTY CHOCOLATES...

There is something about nuts and chocolate – any nuts and any chocolate, milk, white or dark! They are so stunningly delicious together.

80g caster sugar
30g water
250g Brazil nuts
1 quantity of tempered dark chocolate
  (see pages 32–33)
50g cocoa powder, for dusting

Place the sugar and water in a medium pan and bring to the boil, stirring to dissolve the sugar. Add the nuts, then stir constantly over a medium heat until the water has evaporated and the nuts are a light brown colour; they should not be too sticky. Remove from the heat. Tip the nuts out on to a piece of baking parchment and leave to cool.

Pour 100g of the tempered dark chocolate on to the nuts, stirring them with your hand as you pour to coat them evenly with the chocolate. Repeat this process with more chocolate until all the nuts are covered in a 1mm-thick layer of chocolate (you will probably need about 300g of the tempered chocolate). Dust them with cocoa powder to finish and leave to set.

nutty

...HAZELNUT PRALINE CHOCOLATE SPREAD...

A couple of years ago Louise was intrigued to see a huge pile of chocolate spread
on the floor at the Basle Art Fair for the princely sum of 48,000 euros.
It was by the artist, Thomas Rentmeister, and caused quite a stir.
This is a super-sophisticated, glamorous Melt version of the world's most popular
chocolate spread. It's perfect as an after-school snack for little ones – simply spread on to
two Rich Tea biscuits, sandwich them together and serve with a glass of cold milk.

Makes 3 x 250g jars

500g praline paste, at room
   temperature
125g dark chocolate, melted
   (see page 28)
125g unsalted butter, softened
10g hazelnut oil

Place all the ingredients in a mixing
bowl and stir thoroughly with a spatula
until they are well combined.

Transfer to 3 cold sterilised jars (see
below) and seal with the lids. Store in a
cool place and use within 3 weeks.

To sterilise glass jars
Preheat the oven to 120°C/Gas Mark $^1/_2$.
Wash the jars and lids in hot soapy
water. Boil a kettle and pour the boiling
water over the jars and lids. Place them
in a roasting tray and put them in the
oven for about 15 minutes, until dry.
Alternatively you can sterilise jars by
putting them through a dishwasher
cycle.

...HAZELNUT SLAB...

An easy recipe that tastes completely and utterly divine.
Hazelnuts and chocolate – life can't get much better than this!

100g hazelnuts
1 quantity of tempered milk chocolate
or tempered dark chocolate (see
pages 32–33)

Preheat the oven to 120°C/Gas Mark $^1/_2$.
Line a baking sheet with a piece of
baking parchment.

Roast the hazelnuts in the oven for
about 10 minutes, until they are lightly
coloured. Set aside to cool.

Place the cooled nuts in a bowl and
add 200g of the tempered chocolate
(you won't need the rest of the
chocolate but it keeps well). Mix well
and spread on to the baking parchment
in a layer about 1cm thick (the same
height as the hazelnuts). Leave to set in
the fridge. Break into chunks to serve.

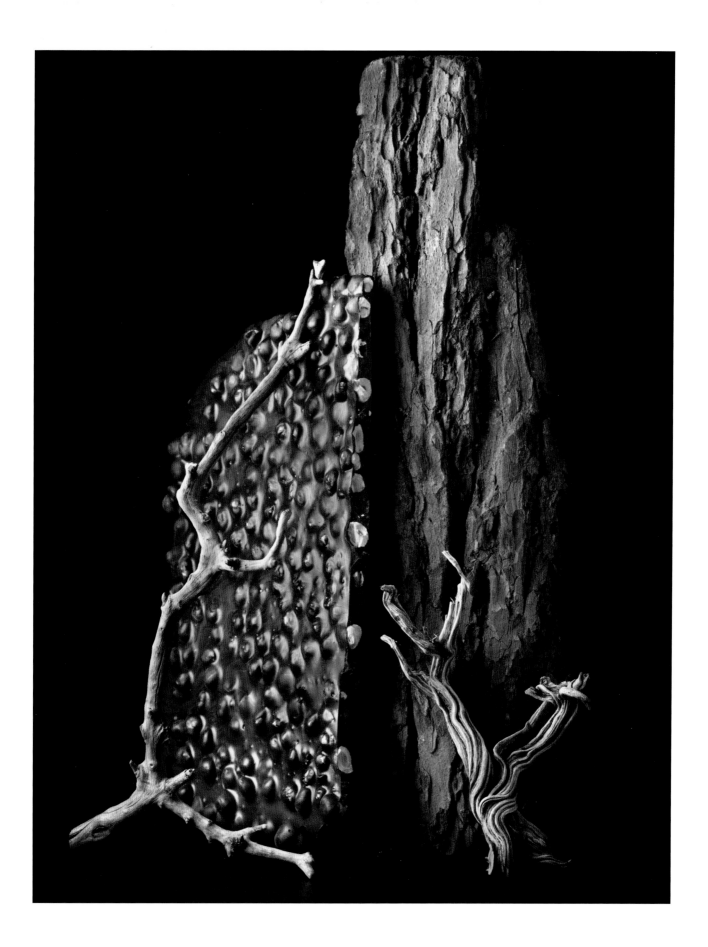

...PISTACHIO
MILK CHOCOLATES...

Pistachios are sexy and exotic with chocolate. Both their flavour and their vibrant green colour make this such a good combination – worth making for a special treat. Although pistachios are expensive, a strong impact can be created with just a small amount.

Makes about 64

50g pistachio nuts, finely chopped, plus
   extra to decorate
200g marzipan
tempered milk chocolate, for dipping
   (see pages 32–33)

For the milk chocolate ganache
150g milk chocolate, finely chopped
100g double or whipping cream
10g liquid glucose
15g unsalted butter, cut into small
   cubes

Line a 20 x 20cm baking tray with baking parchment.

Knead the pistachio nuts into the marzipan. Roll the marzipan out with a rolling pin to fit the base of the baking tray, then put it in the tray.

For the ganache, put the milk chocolate in a bowl. Put the cream and glucose in a small pan and bring just to boiling point. Remove from the heat, pour on to the milk chocolate and stir gently from the middle to emulsify. Check on a digital thermometer that the temperature is no higher than 45°C, then stir in the butter until well combined. Pour the ganache on top of the marzipan layer and tap the tray on a work surface to smooth the top. Leave overnight in a cool place, but not the fridge.

Invert the tray to remove the chocolate and marzipan block, then peel off the parchment. Spread a thin, even layer of tempered chocolate over the marzipan with a palette knife or, if you prefer, apply the chocolate with a pastry brush. Leave until set, then cut into small rectangles or squares. Use a dipping fork to dip into tempered chocolate (see page 43), then decorate with chopped pistachios.

...MARZIPAN LOGS...

Marzipan – you either love it or loathe it. For fans, it is very evocative of Christmas.
The soft, paste-like texture is perfect for coating in tempered chocolate.

Makes 20

grated zest of 1 orange
150g marzipan
5g ground mixed spice
30g candied orange peel, finely
  chopped
tempered dark chocolate, for dipping
  (see pages 32–33)

Spread the orange zest out on a baking tray and leave in a warm place, such as an airing cupboard or a warm room, for a day to dry; it should be dry enough to crumble to a powder between your fingers.

Put the marzipan, mixed spice and candied orange peel in a bowl and knead together well. Roll the marzipan into a 1.5cm-diameter sausage shape. Cut it into 3cm lengths and leave them to dry overnight on baking parchment.

Dip the marzipan pieces in the tempered chocolate (see page 43), place on baking parchment and sprinkle over the dried orange zest. Leave to set.

...CHESTNUT AND CHOCOLATE PUDDING...

This dessert has the weight and taste normally delivered by a seriously stodgy pudding but it is in fact made with chestnuts, milk, crème fraîche and very little sugar. The recipe is based on one from Michel Montignac, who created the Montignac Method – a weight-loss diet that relies on the glycemic index. Montignac uses fructose instead of brown sugar. Serve in skinny slices, with pouring cream.

Serves 8

200g dark chocolate (at least 66 per
    cent cocoa solids), chopped
200g peeled, prepared fresh or
    vacuum-packed chestnuts
100ml full-fat milk
1 vanilla pod, slit open lengthwise, or
    1 teaspoon best-quality vanilla extract
100ml crème fraîche
25g soft brown sugar
single cream, to serve

Line a 20 x 10cm loaf tin with cling film.

Put the chopped chocolate in a heatproof bowl and place in a low oven (about 50°C) for 10–15 minutes, until melted, stirring once or twice.

Meanwhile, place the chestnuts in a small pan with the milk and split vanilla pod (or extract) and cook gently for 15–20 minutes, until the chestnuts are softened. Remove the vanilla pod and blitz the chestnuts and milk in a food processor or blender until smooth (alternatively, you could mash them with a potato masher).

Slowly pour the melted chocolate into the chestnut purée and stir until well mixed. Stir in the crème fraîche and soft brown sugar. Spoon the mixture into the loaf tin and chill for at least 3 hours.

To serve, tap the pudding out of the tin and remove the cling film. Slice into slivers and drizzle with cream.

...COCONUT SQUARES...

These are full of dreamy childhood memories – the unforgettable marriage of coconut and chocolate. This is a very glamorous version, and it can really cast you out to coastal climes. The milk chocolate ganache is layered with a moist coconut layer, creating what is arguably one of our all-time favourite chocolates.

Makes about 64

150g white chocolate, finely chopped
100g coconut cream
1 teaspoon lime juice
10g liquid glucose
10g cocoa butter
25g desiccated coconut, plus a little extra to decorate
tempered dark chocolate, for dipping (see pages 32–33)

For the milk chocolate ganache
150g milk chocolate (40 per cent cocoa solids), finely chopped
100g double cream
10g liquid glucose
15g unsalted butter, cut into small cubes

Line a 20cm square baking tin with baking parchment.

Put the chopped white chocolate in a bowl. Put the coconut cream, lime juice and glucose in a small pan and bring just to boiling point, then remove from the heat and pour on to the chocolate. Stir gently from the middle to emulsify. Check on a digital thermometer that the temperature is no higher than 45°C, then stir in the cocoa butter and desiccated coconut.

Pour the chocolate mixture into the prepared tin. Tap the tin on the work surface to smooth the top, then leave at cool room temperature for at least 6 hours or overnight to set.

For the ganache, put the milk chocolate in a bowl. Put the cream and glucose in a small pan and bring just to boiling point. Remove from the heat, pour on to the milk chocolate and stir gently from the centre to emulsify. Check on a digital thermometer that the temperature is no higher than 45°C, then add the butter and stir until melted. Pour the ganache on to the coconut layer and tap the tray on the worktop to smooth the surface. Leave overnight in a cool place, but not the fridge.

Invert the tray to remove the chocolate and coconut block, then peel off the parchment. Spread a thin, even layer of tempered chocolate (about 2 tablespoons) over the top with a palette knife or, if you prefer, apply the chocolate with a pastry brush. Leave until set, then cut into small rectangles or squares. Use a dipping fork to dip them into tempered chocolate (see page 43), then decorate with a little desiccated coconut.

...*f*ruit
and tr*o*pical
tw*i*sts...

...CHOCOLATE TART WITH BLOOD ORANGE MARMALADE...

A good chocolate tart can be served as pudding, smart dessert or afternoon treat or given as a delicious gift. The citrus tang of orange goes so well with chocolate, be it milk, dark or white. Use a chocolate with a robust character for this tart, such as Valrhona Extra Bitter (61 per cent cocoa solids content), which uses a blend of Criollos and Forasteros beans from a variety of regions. Or make it really special with a Melt single-origin bar like Smoke, which has an earthy, liquorice quality with smoky notes.

Serves 6–8

200g dark chocolate (at least 60 per cent cocoa solids)
150g unsalted butter, cut into cubes
2 organic eggs
3 organic egg yolks
40g golden caster sugar
whipped cream, to serve

For the sweet pastry
180g unsalted butter, cut into cubes
2 medium organic egg yolks
70g icing sugar
230g plain flour

For the blood orange marmalade
225g golden caster sugar
60ml blood orange juice (use ordinary oranges if blood oranges are not available)
30g grated blood orange zest (just grate on a grater or take off strips with a peeler, avoiding too much pith)
185ml water

First make the pastry. Place the butter, egg yolks and icing sugar in a food processor and mix until combined. Add the flour and mix again until it forms a ball. Wrap in baking parchment or cling film and chill for at least 2 hours.

Meanwhile, make the blood orange marmalade. Put all the ingredients in a small pan and heat gently, stirring until the sugar has dissolved. Simmer over a low to medium heat for about 20 minutes, until reduced to a syrup; don't let it get too sticky, as it will thicken on cooling. Remove from the heat and leave to cool.

Preheat the oven to 180°C/Gas Mark 4.

Cut the pastry in half (you will only need half for this recipe but you can wrap the other piece up and freeze it). Grate the pastry directly into a 22cm loose-based tart tin, using the coarse side of the grater. Push the gratings around and into place along the bottom and up the sides of the tin, closing all the gaps (a laborious process but the resulting pastry is meltingly crumbly). Line with a sheet of baking parchment, fill with baking beans or rice and bake blind for about 15 minutes, until light golden.

Remove the paper and beans and return the pastry case to the oven for another 5 minutes. Remove from the oven and leave to cool. Reduce the oven temperature to 50°C.

To make the filling, break the chocolate into pieces and place in a heatproof bowl with the cubed butter. Place in the oven for 10–15 minutes, until melted, stirring gently once or twice.

Increase the oven temperature to 180°C/Gas Mark 4. Meanwhile, beat the eggs, egg yolks and sugar together until well combined. Add the warm chocolate and butter mixture and mix until just combined. Pour the mixture into the pastry case and bake for 10 minutes maximum, until the surface of the tart has turned matt and lost its gloss. Leave to cool to room temperature.

Serve each slice of chocolate tart with a spoonful of lightly whipped cream and a drizzle of marmalade.

...CASSIS CYLINDERS...

It's fun making different-shaped chocolates with different finishes. These cylinder shapes can be used for any ganache. You'll need a piping bag and some patience, as they need at least six hours to dry before being coated in a layer of chocolate.

Make 45

70g blackcurrant purée (see page 42)
25g raspberry purée (see page 42)
35g caster sugar
15g liquid glucose
90g milk chocolate (35–40 per cent cocoa solids), finely chopped
90g dark chocolate (66 per cent cocoa solids), finely chopped
40g unsalted butter, cut into small cubes
tempered dark chocolate, for dipping (see pages 32–33)

Put the blackcurrant and raspberry purées in a small pan, add the sugar and glucose and bring to the boil. Remove from the heat.

Put the chopped milk and dark chocolate in a bowl and add the fruit purée. Stir gently from the middle to emulsify. Check on a digital thermometer that the temperature is no higher than 45°C, then stir in the butter until combined. Leave in a cool place until firm enough to pipe.

To make sure the ganache is the right consistency, stir well – this will give an even texture and the air that is introduced will help to thicken the mixture. Fit a 15mm plain nozzle into a piping bag and fill it with the ganache. Pipe lengths on to a baking sheet lined with baking parchment; the mixture should be thick enough to come out in a perfect cylinder shape rather than flatten underneath where it meets the parchment. Leave in a cool place (but not the fridge) for at least 6 hours to firm up

Cut the ganache into 3cm pieces. Use a dipping fork to coat them in tempered dark chocolate (see page 43).

...MANGO AND PASSIONFRUIT PATE DE FRUIT...

Pâté de fruit is essentially a jelly, possessing jewel-like colours and traditionally finished with a dusting of white sugar. We use it to bring flavour to chocolates, layered with ganache and then enrobed. Stored in an airtight container with a dusting of caster sugar, these should keep for up to 1 month.

Makes 100

250g passionfruit purée (see page 42)
240g caster sugar
100g liquid glucose
14g pectin
6g lemon juice
tempered dark chocolate, for dipping
   (see pages 32–33)

For the mango ganache
330g milk chocolate (40 per cent cocoa
   solids), finely chopped
120g mango purée (see page 42)
40g passionfruit purée (see page 42)
50g liquid glucose
40g unsalted butter, cut into small
   cubes

Line a 22.5 x 34cm baking tin with baking parchment.

Put the 250g passionfruit purée in a pan and bring to the boil. Add 200g of the sugar and the glucose, stir well to dissolve the sugar and bring back to the boil. Mix the remaining sugar with the pectin and add to the pan. When the mixture reaches 112°C on a sugar thermometer, remove from the heat, add the lemon juice and stir well. Pour in to the baking tin. Leave to cool and set.

For the mango ganache, put the chocolate in a bowl. Put the mango purée, passionfruit purée and glucose in a small pan, bring to the boil and pour on to the chopped chocolate. Stir gently from the middle to emulsify. Check on a digital thermometer that the temperature is no higher than 45°C, then stir in the butter until combined. Pour the ganache over the pâté de fruit in the tin and leave overnight in a cool place, but not the fridge.

Invert the tray to remove the mixture, then peel off the baking parchment. Spread a thin, even layer of the tempered chocolate over the top with a palette knife – or, if you prefer, apply the chocolate with a pastry brush. Leave until set, then cut into small rectangles or squares. Use a dipping fork to coat the pieces in tempered chocolate (see page 43). If you like, you can rest a piece of patterned acetate on top of the dipped chocolates and leave until set, to create a pattern.

...fruit and tropical twists...

...BANANA, COCONUT AND PASSIONFRUIT BONBONS...

This Academy of Chocolate award winner will appeal to the sweet-toothed amongst us.
It has a wonderful fruitiness and texture – a happy chocolate, sweet and sunny.
You can experiment with different finishes instead of the dacquoise: try crushed
freeze-dried raspberries mixed with an equal quantity of icing sugar to create a 'blush';
crystallised mint leaves (see Suppliers, page 183) or even a touch of ground black pepper.

Makes 50

130g double cream
50g liquid glucose
40g banana pureé (see page 42)
35g passionfruit purée (see page 42)
60g coconut cream
100g caster sugar
70g white chocolate, finely chopped
50g unsalted butter, cut into small
  cubes
50 dark chocolate shells (see page 43)
tempered dark chocolate, for rolling
  (see pages 32–33)
crushed Dacquoise (see opposite), for
  dusting

In a small pan, bring the double cream, glucose, fruit purées and coconut cream to the boil, then remove from the heat.

Put a small heavy-based pan over a low heat and leave until hot. Add the sugar and leave until melted, stirring very gently from time to time if it looks as if it's about to burn at the edges. Once it's melted, raise the heat and let it boil until it becomes a dark golden caramel. Remove from the heat and add the cream mixture – be careful, as it will splutter. Stir until smooth.

Put the chopped chocolate in a bowl and pour on the caramel mixture. Stir gently from the middle to emulsify. Check on a digital thermometer that the temperature is no higher than 45°C, then stir in the butter until combined. When the mixture is at body temperature, pipe it into the chocolate shells. Set aside in a cool place (but not the fridge) for the filling to firm up.

Seal the chocolates and roll them in the tempered dark chocolate as described on page 43. Dust with crushed Dacquoise.

To make Dacquoise

Makes enough to cover 150–200 small chocolates

Place 100g sifted icing sugar, 80g ground almonds and 20g desiccated coconut in a bowl, mix together and set aside. Put 100g egg whites in a large bowl and whisk until aerated. Add 20g caster sugar and whisk until the whites form soft peaks. Add another 20g caster sugar and whisk until just before the mixture forms stiff peaks. Add about half the almond mixture and fold it in, then fold in the rest.

Spread the mixture on a baking tray lined with baking parchment in a 5mm-thick layer. Bake in an oven preheated to 160°C/Gas Mark 3 for 20–30 minutes, until completely dry; it will colour lightly but should not go brown. Transfer to a wire rack and leave to cool.

Peel off the paper and crush the dacquoise to a very fine powder – you can do this in a food processor. Store in the freezer for up to a month and just take out what you need.

115

...fruit and tropical twists...

...BANANA CARAMEL BONBONS...

When Louise was walking towards Melt one morning, she smelled a glorious, sweet banana
aroma wafting in the air and knew that the kitchen was making this chocolate.
Banana and chocolate has a pleasing, youthful quality, sweet and comforting.
In our opinion, milk chocolate is the best to pair with banana.

116

Makes 40

90g double cream
50g banana purée (see page 42)
50g caster sugar
90g milk chocolate (35–40 per cent
    cocoa solids), finely chopped
20g cocoa butter, melted
20g unsalted butter, cut into small
    cubes
40 milk chocolate shells (see page 43)
tempered milk chocolate, for rolling (see
    pages 32–33)
a few dried banana pieces, crushed, to
    decorate

Place the double cream and banana
purée in a small pan, bring to the boil
and remove from the heat.

Put a heavy-based pan over a low heat
and leave until hot. Add the sugar and
leave until melted, stirring very gently
from time to time if it looks as if it's
about to burn at the edges. Once it's
melted, raise the heat and let it boil until
it becomes a dark golden caramel.
Remove from the heat and add the
cream and banana purée mixture – be
careful, as it will splutter. Stir until
smooth.

Put the chopped chocolate in a bowl
and pour on the melted cocoa butter,
followed by the caramel mixture. Stir
gently from the middle to emulsify.
Check on a digital thermometer that the
temperature is no higher than 45°C,
then stir in the butter until combined.

When the mixture has cooled to body
temperature, pipe it into the chocolate
shells. Set aside in a cool place (but not
the fridge) for the filling to firm up.

Seal the chocolates and roll them in the
tempered milk chocolate as described
on page 43. Sprinkle the top of each
chocolate with crushed dried banana.

...PASSIONFRUIT BONBONS...

The sweet, rich, luscious and highly perfumed passionfruit takes the leading role in this bonbon. The milk chocolate will simply round off the intense, fruity hit with a little creamy sweetness.

Make 50

170g passionfruit purée (see page 42)
85g caster sugar
35g liquid glucose
135g milk chocolate (40% per cent cocoa solids), finely chopped
25g unsalted butter, cut into small cubes
50 milk chocolate shells (see page 43)
tempered dark chocolate, for rolling (see pages 32–33)
$^1/_2$ teaspoon coffee extract

Place the purée, sugar and glucose in a small pan and bring to the boil, then remove from the heat.

Place the chopped chocolate in a bowl and pour the fruit mixture over. Stir gently from the middle to emulsify. Check on a digital thermometer that the temperature is no higher than 45°C, then stir in the butter until well combined. When the mixture is at body temperature, pipe it into the chocolate shells. Set aside in a cool place (but not the fridge) to set.

Combine the tempered dark chocolate and coffee extract. Seal the chocolates and roll them in the tempered chocolate as described on page 43.

...fruit and tropical twists...

...BILL GRANGER'S HONEYCOMB CHOCOLATES...

We were thrilled to work with the chef, Bill Granger, whose signature dessert at his restaurant in Japan is honeycomb and banana. Chika's wonderful adaptation is this honeycomb and banana crunch. Honeycomb is really fun to make, although you need to be careful when you add the bicarbonate of soda and the mixture starts to bubble volcanically. Any leftover honeycomb can be kept for nibbles or mixed through tempered chocolate for a quick treat.

Makes 30

1 quantity of tempered dark chocolate (66 per cent cocoa solids) (see pages 32–33)
120g praline paste
30g freeze-dried banana slices
tempered milk chocolate, for decorating (see pages 32–33)

For the honeycomb
115g caster sugar
150g water
15g runny honey
½ tsp bicarbonate of soda

To make the honeycomb, put the sugar, water and honey in a heavy-based pan and heat gently, stirring to dissolve the sugar. Raise the heat, bring to the boil and cook, without stirring, until the temperature reaches 154°C on a sugar thermometer. Remove the pan from the heat, add the bicarbonate of soda and stir gently – be careful, as the mixture will foam and increase in volume. Pour the mixture on to a baking sheet lined with baking parchment and leave to cool and set. Crush the honeycomb into small pieces.

Mix 100g of the tempered dark chocolate with the praline in a bowl. Add 30g of the crushed honeycomb and the freeze-dried banana and mix very well. Pour the mixture on to a baking tray lined with baking parchment and leave to set until firm.

Put the chocolate and honeycomb mixture between 2 sheets of baking parchment and roll it with a rolling pin to a 3mm thickness. Cut it into 2cm x 3cm rectangles. Use a dipping fork to coat them in the tempered milk chocolate (see page 43), then drop dots of the remaining tempered dark chocolate over with another fork and rub gently with the fork in a circular movement to make a marble effect.

...fruit and tropical twists...

...RHUBARB AND RASPBERRY PAVLOVA...

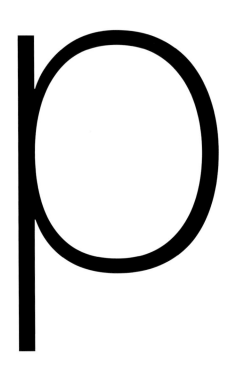

A pavlova never fails to seduce, especially this one, which has little surprises tucked within the meringue – chunks of date and dark chocolate to create a wonderfully rich texture. The pinky hues of the rhubarb and raspberry make it as pretty as a blushing bride. Pavlovas look most impressive when they're large, like this one – so perfect for a party.

...melt...

Serves 8

5 organic egg whites
230g golden caster sugar
100g dark chocolate (at least 60 per
    cent cocoa solids)
4 soft dried dates, chopped
300ml double cream

For the rhubarb and raspberry topping

4 sticks of rhubarb, cut into 3cm
    lengths
50g golden caster sugar
500g fresh raspberries
80ml sweet wine (optional)

Line a large baking sheet with baking parchment. Preheat the oven to 110°C/ Gas Mark ¼.

Put the egg whites in a large bowl and whisk with an electric beater until doubled in volume and verging on stiff, but still with a little wobble. Continue to whisk while gradually adding the sugar; the volume will continue to increase and the whites will turn glossy. Stop whisking when the mixture is glossy and stiff.

Bash the chocolate using a pestle and mortar, or chop it on a board, to make small nuggets. Gently stir and streak the chocolate and dates through the meringue.

Spoon the meringue carefully on to the baking parchment in a large circle, about 5cm thick. Cook for 2 hours, then turn the oven off and leave the pavlova to cool in the oven with the door ajar. Be careful not to overcook the meringue or the dates will get too hard – you want to keep their delectable squishiness!

Meanwhile, place the rhubarb and sugar in a small pan and cook over a low heat for 20 minutes or until tender. Transfer the rhubarb to a bowl with a slotted spoon. Add the raspberries and sweet wine or a dash of water to the pan and cook over a low heat for 10 minutes. Return the rhubarb to the pan, stir through gently and leave to cool.

Whip the double cream until it has thickened slightly, then smooth it over the pavlova. Top with the cooled rhubarb and raspberries and their juices.

...FRUIT MARSHMALLOWS...

These beautiful white, pillow-soft marshmallows are extremely popular. They are as light as air and not too sweet. The natural dried fruit pieces explode with fruity bursts, and it's fun to nibble off the chocolate. Two hundred marshmallows might seem like a lot, but this is the perfect recipe to make if you are thinking of sweet treats for a children's party or lovely homemade gifts for all ages, especially at Christmas. At Melt we make these with invert sugar paste, which you can track down on the internet but you usually have to buy it in large quantities. So we've adapted the recipe here to use glucose, which works almost as well.

Makes about 200

22g gelatine leaves
105g liquid glucose
340g caster sugar
120g water
50g freeze-dried fruit (e.g. banana, passionfruit, raspberries or strawberries), crumbled into small pieces
icing sugar, for dusting
tempered dark chocolate, for dipping (see pages 32–33)

Line a 30 x 45cm baking tray with baking parchment.

Put the gelatine leaves in a bowl of cold water and leave to soak for about 5 minutes, until soft. Remove from the bowl, gently squeeze out excess water and place the gelatine in the bowl of a freestanding electric mixer fitted with a whisk attachment. Add the glucose.

Put the sugar and water in a heavy-based pan and bring slowly to the boil, stirring to dissolve the sugar. Boil, without stirring, until it reaches 110°C on a sugar thermometer. As soon as it does, switch the electric mixer on to a medium speed and slowly pour in the sugar syrup down the side of the bowl, whisking all the time. After the sugar syrup has all been added, continue to whisk on a medium speed until the mixture is white and fluffy and has greatly increased in volume; it should be at body temperature. Reduce the speed to slow and add the freeze-dried fruit. Mix until just combined.

Transfer the marshmallow to the lined baking tray with a spatula and then smooth the top with a palette knife. Leave to set at room temperature for about 30 minutes.

Dust the marshmallow quite heavily with icing sugar, turn on to a chopping board, then peel off the paper – you will probably need to apply heat to do this (a hairdryer works well!). Dust with more icing sugar and cut into 2.5cm squares with a sharp knife dusted with icing sugar. Dust off excess icing sugar and then dip the squares into the tempered chocolate to half-coat them, or simply drizzle with chocolate, as per the picture.

These keep for up to 3 weeks if stored in an airtight container.

...CANDIED ORANGE THINS...

This is a fun chocolate technique to try out. The chocolate is squashed between two layers of acetate to create pretty, slightly irregular-shaped discs and the finish is very shiny and appealing. Orange and chocolate is such a classic combination. These would make a really pretty Christmas gift.

Makes 30

30g candied orange peel, very finely chopped
3g ground mixed spice
1 quantity of tempered milk chocolate (see pages 32–33)

Put a 20 x 30cm sheet of acetate on a chopping board. Snip the end off a disposable piping bag to leave a 7mm hole.

Mix the candied orange peel and mixed spice with 250g of the chocolate and pour into the piping bag (you won't need the remaining chocolate for this recipe but it keeps well). Squeeze the chocolate on to the acetate in rounds about 3cm in diameter, leaving them very well spaced out. Carefully place a second acetate sheet on top of the chocolate, then cover with a chopping board and leave for about 10 minutes, until the chocolates are approximately 2mm thick. Leave to set and allow 6 hours before removing the acetate, to ensure beautiful, shining chocolate.

...RASPBERRY AND DARK CHOCOLATE PRESERVE...

This sells very well at Melt. It is a versatile spread that is good
as a filling for a plain sponge cake or spread on warm croissants in the morning.

Makes 2 x 350g jars

500g raspberry purée (see page 42)
250g caster sugar
6g pectin
125g dark chocolate (66 per cent
   cocoa solids), finely chopped

Put the raspberry purée in a small pan
and heat gently until it reaches body
temperature, then add the sugar and
pectin. Stir well, increase the heat and
cook until it reaches 105°C on a sugar
thermometer.

Put the chocolate in a heatproof bowl
and pour on the raspberry mixture.
Stir gently to emulsify. Pour it into cold
sterilised jars (see page 99) and seal.
The preserve should keep for up to
3 weeks stored at cool room
temperature.

...TROPICAL PRESERVE...

Any excuse to put chocolate in practically everything – this is why at Melt we have created a number of very versatile preserves. You can use them as a filling for cakes, spread on brioche or croissants or added to Greek yogurt or ice cream. This recipe is particularly fragrant.

Makes 2 x 350g jars

150g passionfruit purée (see page 42)
150g lychee purée (see page 42)
200g mango purée (see page 42)
250g caster sugar
6g pectin
125g dark chocolate (64 per cent cocoa solids), finely chopped

Put the fruit purées in a small pan and warm until they reach body temperature, then add the sugar and pectin. Stir well, increase the heat and cook until the mixture reaches 105°C on a sugar thermometer.

Put the chocolate in a heatproof bowl and pour on the fruit mixture. Stir gently to emulsify. Pour it into cold sterilised jars (see page 99) and seal. The preserve should keep for up to 3 weeks stored at cool room temperature.

...BLACKBERRY AND CINNAMON BARS...

This recipe comes from our extensive collection of flavoured chocolate bars, which we make by hand in all shapes and sizes. The blackberry adds a fruity tang and brings the milk chocolate alive, while the cinnamon adds warmth. Like many of our other recipes, these cute little bars make the perfect gift. They can happily be kept at room temperature in dry conditions for at least six months without any detriment to flavour – although I doubt very much that they would ever sit around for this long! You will need ten 50g bar moulds.

Makes 10 x 50g bars

1 quantity of tempered milk chocolate (see pages 32–33)
15g freeze-dried blackberries, ground to a powder
20g ground cinnamon

Polish ten 50g bar moulds with cotton wool (this makes the bars shiny). Cut the tip off a disposable piping bag to leave an 8mm hole.

Mix the tempered milk chocolate with the blackberry and cinnamon powders. Pour them into the piping bag and pipe into the prepared moulds, filling them to the top. Leave in the fridge to set completely.

Invert the moulds to remove the chocolate bars, then wrap in baking parchment.

...OLIVE CARAMEL BONBONS...

Inspired by the beautiful black olive caramel in Jason Atherton's book, *Maze: The Cookbook* (Quadrille, 2008), we experimented, tweaked and played with olive tapenade to create this Academy of Chocolate award-winning, adventurous chocolate.

Makes 60

250g double cream
35g full-fat milk
seeds from $1/2$ vanilla pod
50g liquid glucose
250g caster sugar
25g unsalted butter, cut into small
   cubes
25g black olive tapenade
60 dark chocolate shells (see page 43)
tempered dark chocolate, for rolling
   (see pages 32–33)

Put the cream, milk and vanilla seeds in a small pan, bring just to boiling point, then remove from the heat and set aside.

Put the glucose in a heavy-based pan and place over a high heat. When it begins to bubble, add a little sugar and stir until melted. Keep adding the sugar until it is all used up, then raise the heat and boil without stirring until you have a golden brown caramel. Remove from the heat, add the warm cream mixture and stir until smooth. Stir in the butter until completely combined and add the tapenade. Set aside to cool.

Cut the tip off a disposable piping bag to leave a 3mm hole and transfer the mixture to the bag. Pipe the mixture into the chocolate shells. Seal the shells with tempered dark chocolate, then roll them in the chocolate to coat (see page 43).

...RHUBARB AND LEMON VERBENA SQUARES...

Rhubarb tends to have a rather old-fashioned reputation, but paired here with lemon verbena in a white chocolate ganache it really does take on a truly modern guise. This is a wonderful example of expressing a very traditional, British flavour in a contemporary way through chocolate.

Makes about 60

tempered dark chocolate, for dipping (see page 43)

For the lemon verbena and white chocolate ganache
125g double cream
15g liquid glucose
10g dried lemon verbena leaves
150g white chocolate (35 per cent cocoa solids), finely chopped
30g cocoa butter, finely chopped
15g unsalted butter, cut into small cubes

For the rhubarb and chocolate ganache
50g dark chocolate (66% per cent cocoa solids), finely chopped
50g milk chocolate (40% per cent cocoa solids), finely chopped
125g rhubarb purée (see page 42)
25g caster sugar
20g liquid glucose
5g cocoa butter
20g unsalted butter, cut into small cubes

Line a 20cm square baking tin with baking parchment.

For the lemon verbena and white chocolate ganache, place the double cream and glucose in a small pan, bring to the boil, then remove from the heat. Add the lemon verbena leaves and set aside to infuse for 1 hour.

Put the chopped white chocolate and cocoa butter into a bowl. Remove the leaves from the cream mixture and bring the infused cream to the boil again, then strain through a fine sieve on to the chocolate. Stir gently from the middle to emulsify. Check on a digital thermometer that the temperature is no higher than 45°C, then stir in the butter until combined. Pour into the prepared tray and set aside in a cool place (but not the fridge) to set.

To make the rhubarb and chocolate ganache, put the dark and milk chocolate in a bowl. Put the rhubarb purée in a pan and place over a medium heat. Bring to boiling point, then remove from the heat.

Put the sugar and glucose in a small pan over a high heat and cook, stirring, until the sugar has dissolved. Continue to cook, without stirring, until it turns golden. Remove from the heat and pour in the rhubarb purée a little at time, stirring until well combined. Pass through a fine sieve on to the chopped chocolate. Stir gently from the middle to emulsify. Check on a digital thermometer that the temperature is no higher than 45°C, then stir in the cocoa butter and unsalted butter until combined. Pour the mixture over the set lemon verbena ganache. Leave in a cool place, but not the fridge, for at least 6 hours or overnight, until the ganache is fully set.

Invert the tray to remove the mixture, then peel off the parchment. Spread a thin, even layer of the tempered chocolate over the top with a palette knife – or, if you prefer, apply the chocolate with a pastry brush. Leave until set, then cut into small rectangles about 2cm x 3cm. Use a dipping fork to coat them in tempered chocolate (see page 43), then leave to set.

...blossoms, leaves and roots...

...FENNEL, GINGER AND WHITE CHOCOLATE BISCOTTI...

These little biscuits can accommodate myriad flavour combinations, depending on what you have in your cupboard. Soft dried apricots work well with the fennel seeds; you could also try date and pine nut or cranberry and spice. They are equally good for morning coffee or after dinner with a small glass of sweet wine, such as the Austrian Samling by Merry Widows. Try to buy organic crystallised ginger. It is less sweet and has a really good heat.

136

Makes 12–16

85g light muscovado sugar
1 organic egg
150g plain flour, plus extra for dusting
$1/_2$ teaspoon baking powder
2 teaspoons fennel seeds
60g crystallised ginger, chopped
100g white chocolate, chopped

Preheat the oven to 180°C/Gas Mark 4. Line a baking tray with baking parchment.

Place the sugar and egg in a bowl and whisk until light and thickened. Sift the flour and baking powder over the mixture. Add the fennel seeds and chopped ginger and mix well to form a paste.

Liberally flour a work surface and your hands. Turn out the paste and mould it into a log shape about 5cm thick. Place the log on the lined baking tray and bake for 10 minutes or until just firm.

Remove from the oven, cut the log across at an angle into pieces about 1.5–2cm thick and lay them flat on the lined baking tray. Return to the oven for 5 minutes, until golden, then leave to cool on the tray.

Put the chopped chocolate in a small heatproof bowl and place in a low oven (about 50°C) for 10–15 minutes, until melted, stirring once or twice.

Dip each biscotti carefully into the melted chocolate, just enough to coat half of the biscuit. Place on a sheet of baking parchment until set.

...ORANGE BLOSSOM SEMIFREDDO WITH RASPBERRIES AND MILK CHOCOLATE...

Orange blossom water is wonderful combined with milk chocolate, especially if cream is also involved. Chocolate is robust enough to stand up to, and even be enhanced by, many flavours and spices, so you can pretty much use the following with gay abandon: nutmeg, vanilla, chilli, cloves and orange blossom.

Serves 8

200g milk chocolate (at least 40 per cent cocoa solids), chopped
3 organic eggs
2 organic egg yolks
220g golden caster sugar
450ml double cream
1 tablespoon orange blossom water
250g raspberries

Line a 1kg loaf tin with cling film.

Put the chocolate in a heatproof bowl and place in a low oven (about 50°C) for 15 minutes or until melted, stirring gently once or twice. Remove and set aside.

Meanwhile, put the eggs, yolks and sugar in a large heatproof bowl and place over a pan of gently simmering water, making sure the water isn't touching the base of the bowl. Whisk with an electric handheld beater for about 5 minutes, until the mixture is thick enough to leave a trail on the surface when the whisk is lifted. Take the bowl off the heat and continue whisking for 4–5 minutes. The mixture should have increased greatly in volume.

Whip the cream in a large mixing bowl until it is just stiff, then gently fold in the orange blossom water and the egg and sugar mixture.

Arrange the raspberries in a single layer in the prepared tin. Pour the mixture on top of the raspberries; it should come to just below the top of the tin. Finally drizzle the melted chocolate across the entire surface of the mixture. The heavier trails will sink, the lighter drizzles will float or just submerge themselves. Freeze for 24 hours.

Remove the semifreddo from the freezer at least 20 minutes before serving to soften slightly. Invert the tin on to a plate, lift it off and gently peel away the clingfilm. Cut into slices to serve.

...blossoms, leaves and roots...

Semi

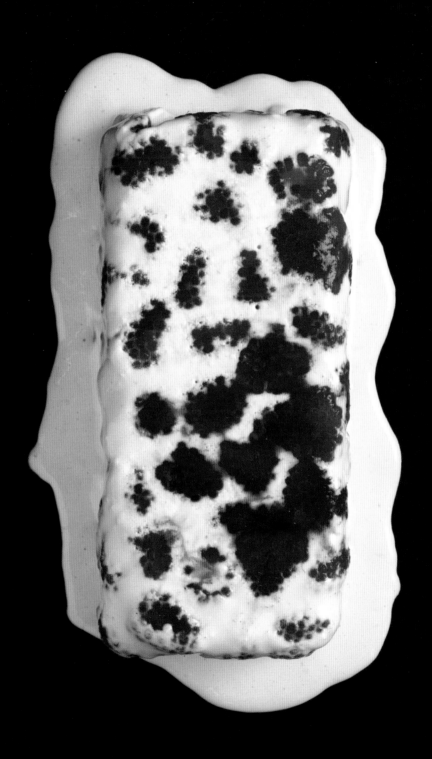

Freddo

...DARK CHOCOLATE AND BEETROOT CAKE...

This divine recipe is not dissimilar in theory to the well-established carrot cake. The beetroot adds texture and moisture rather than any discernible flavour. This version includes a thick, dark chocolate topping. This hard shell contrasts very well with the soft, moist cake, but for speed this is optional and the cake can instead be served warm from the oven. For the topping, I like to use a smoky, earthy, single-estate dark chocolate from São Tomé, an island off the west coast of Africa, which is a chocolate we stock at Melt (also available at other chocolate stores and some supermarkets). Alternatively, use a dark chocolate with at least 60 per cent cocoa solids.

2–3 slices of fresh ginger, approximately 5mm thick
250g raw beetroot, unpeeled
200g unsalted butter, cut into cubes
400g dark chocolate (at least 60 per cent cocoa solids), chopped
5 organic eggs, separated
180g dark soft brown sugar
135g plain flour

Preheat the oven to 180°C/Gas Mark 4. Grease a 20cm round, loose-based cake tin and line the base with baking parchment.

Place the slices of fresh ginger in a measuring jug, pour over 250ml boiling water and set aside to infuse.

Place the beetroot in a pan, cover with plenty of water, bring to the boil and cook for 40–50 minutes, until soft. Drain and leave to cool, then slip off the tops and skin with a paring knife. Quarter the beetroot and blitz in a food processor or blender with 4 tablespoons of the ginger water until very finely chopped but not a complete mush.

Put the butter and 300g of the chocolate in a heatproof bowl and place in a low oven (about 50°C) for 15 minutes, until melted, stirring gently once or twice. Remove and set aside.

Meanwhile, whisk the egg whites until stiff. Take the chocolate and butter out of the oven and stir to amalgamate well. Stir the egg yolks vigorously into the warm chocolate and butter, then stir the sugar in until well combined. Fold this mixture gently into the whisked egg whites. Finally sift the flour and fold it in, followed by the beetroot mixture.

Turn the mixture into the prepared cake tin and bake for 30–40 minutes or until a knife inserted in the centre comes out clean. Remove from the oven and leave to cool in the tin.

To make the topping, melt the remaining chocolate in the turned-off oven. Coat the cake with a thick layer of the melted chocolate and leave to set.

Serve the cake with a blob of mascarpone or whipped cream and a cup of fresh ginger tea.

... melt ...

...FENNEL AND GINGER DISCS...

These are easy and fun to make.
Stacked up in some baking
parchment or cellophane and tied with
a ribbon, these pretty, irregular-shaped
discs make a really lovely gift.
The fennel seeds offer a little crunch.
Generally herbs are not such good
partners with chocolate as spices,
yet it's worth being adventurous.
Dark chocolate with fennel is
really rather good.

Makes 30

30g crystallised ginger, very finely chopped
5g fennel seeds, chopped
1 quantity of tempered milk chocolate (see pages 32–33)

Put a 20 x 30cm sheet of acetate on a chopping board. Snip the end off a disposable piping bag to leave a 7mm hole.

Mix the ginger and fennel with half the chocolate and pour it into the piping bag (you won't need the rest of the chocolate for this recipe but it keeps well). Squeeze the chocolate on to the acetate in rounds about 3cm in diameter, leaving them well spaced out. Carefully place a second acetate sheet on top of the chocolate, then cover with a chopping board and leave for about 10 minutes, until the chocolates are about 2mm thick.

Leave to set, allowing 6 hours before removing the acetate so the chocolates are beautifully shiny.

...blossoms, leaves and roots...

...ROSE RASPBERRY LOG...

Floral flavours can work really well if they are natural and subtle. Rose tastes beautiful with chocolate as long as the rose essence is not synthetic but good quality and you add just enough to give a gentle, fresh, floral flavour.

Makes 50

30g caster sugar
10g liquid glucose
100g raspberry purée (see page 42)
70g milk chocolate (35–40 per cent cocoa solids), finely chopped
110g dark chocolate (66 per cent cocoa solids), finely chopped
50g unsalted butter, cut into small cubes
5 drops of rose essence
tempered dark chocolate, for dipping (see pages 32–33)
crystallised rose petals or dried rose petals, to decorate

Put the sugar, glucose and raspberry purée in a pan and bring to the boil. Remove from the heat. Put the chopped milk and dark chocolate in a bowl and pour the hot fruit purée mixture over. Stir gently from the middle to emulsify. Check on a digital thermometer that the temperature is no higher than 45°C, then stir in the butter until combined. Finally, stir in the rose essence. Leave in a cool place until firm enough to pipe.

To make sure the ganache is the right consistency, stir well – this will give an even texture and the air that is introduced will help to thicken the mixture.

Fit a plain 15mm nozzle into a piping bag and fill it with the ganache. Pipe 30cm lengths on to a baking sheet lined with baking parchment; the mixture should be thick enough to come out in a perfect cylinder shape rather than flatten underneath where it meets the parchment. Leave in a cool place (but not the fridge) for at least 6 hours to set.

Cut the piped lengths into 3cm pieces. Use a dipping fork to coat them in tempered chocolate (see page 43). Place on a sheet of baking parchment, sprinkle with little pieces of rose petal to decorate and leave to set.

...blossoms, leaves and roots...

...pure
and simple...

...CHOCOLATE PANNA COTTA WITH VANILLA SYRUP...

Louise was looking around for ramekins in the kitchen one day when she was making this and stumbled across some egg cups. She decided it would be fun to use them as moulds to make little chocolate 'bosoms' – or little hills for the prudish.

Serves 8

250ml full-fat milk
500ml double cream
60g golden caster sugar
80g dark chocolate (at least 66 per cent cocoa solids), chopped
20g good-quality unsweetened cocoa powder, sifted
1 sachet of powdered gelatine
double cream, to serve

For the vanilla syrup
25g golden caster sugar
50ml water
1 vanilla pod

Put half the milk in a pan with the cream, sugar, chocolate and cocoa powder. Place over a low heat and stir with a wooden spoon, punching out the clumps of cocoa powder, until it is completely smooth.

Heat the rest of the milk in a small pan until it is hot but not boiling. Remove from the heat, sprinkle the gelatine over the top and stir until dissolved. Add to the hot chocolate mixture and stir until thoroughly combined. Strain through a fine sieve into a jug, then pour the mixture into little ramekins, dariole moulds or eggcups. Place in the fridge for 3–4 hours or overnight, until set.

Shortly before serving, make the vanilla syrup. Place the sugar and water in a small pan and heat gently, stirring, until the sugar has melted. Split the vanilla pod in half lengthways and add to the sugar and water. Pummel the pod with a wooden spoon to release the seeds. Heat until the mixture is just coming to the boil, then reduce the heat to as low as possible and bubble gently for about 15 minutes, until the syrup is thick but not too sticky. Leave for 5 minutes to lose some heat but do not let it cool or it will solidify.

Pour the vanilla syrup on to 8 white serving plates so you can see all the lovely seeds. To unmould the panna cottas, loosen the edges with a knife and tap out on to the plates on top of the syrup – if they are still reluctant to come out, dip the moulds into a bowl of hot water for a few seconds. Drizzle some double cream over the panna cotta and serve.

... melt ...

...CHOCOLATE CARAMELS...

This wonderful recipe gives a powerful chocolate hit followed by a deliciously creamy aftertaste. The lecithin helps to emulsify the mixture. You can buy lecithin granules from healthfood shops but if you can't get hold of any, just leave it out – the fat will separate out slightly but the caramels will still taste delicious.

Make about 50

250g double cream
85g milk
4g sea salt
2g bicarbonate of soda
8g lecithin
425g caster sugar
50g liquid glucose
150g water
150g dark chocolate (preferably
    100 per cent cocoa solids, although
    85–90 per cent will do), chopped
200g unsalted butter, cut into cubes

Line a 22cm x 32cm baking tray with baking parchment.

Place the double cream, milk, salt, bicarbonate of soda and lecithin in a pan and bring to the boil, stirring well to dissolve the lecithin. Remove from the heat and set aside.

Put the sugar, glucose and water into a large, heavy-based pan and heat gently, stirring to dissolve the sugar. Raise the heat and cook without stirring until the mixture reaches 145°C on a sugar thermometer.

Reduce the heat to medium and carefully pour the cream mixture into the sugar and glucose mixture, then add the chopped chocolate and butter.

Over a medium heat, stir with a whisk until the mixture reaches 117°C on a sugar thermometer. Remove from the heat and pour the mixture into the lined baking tray. Leave overnight until firm, then cut into 3cm x 4cm rectangles and wrap in squares of baking parchment.

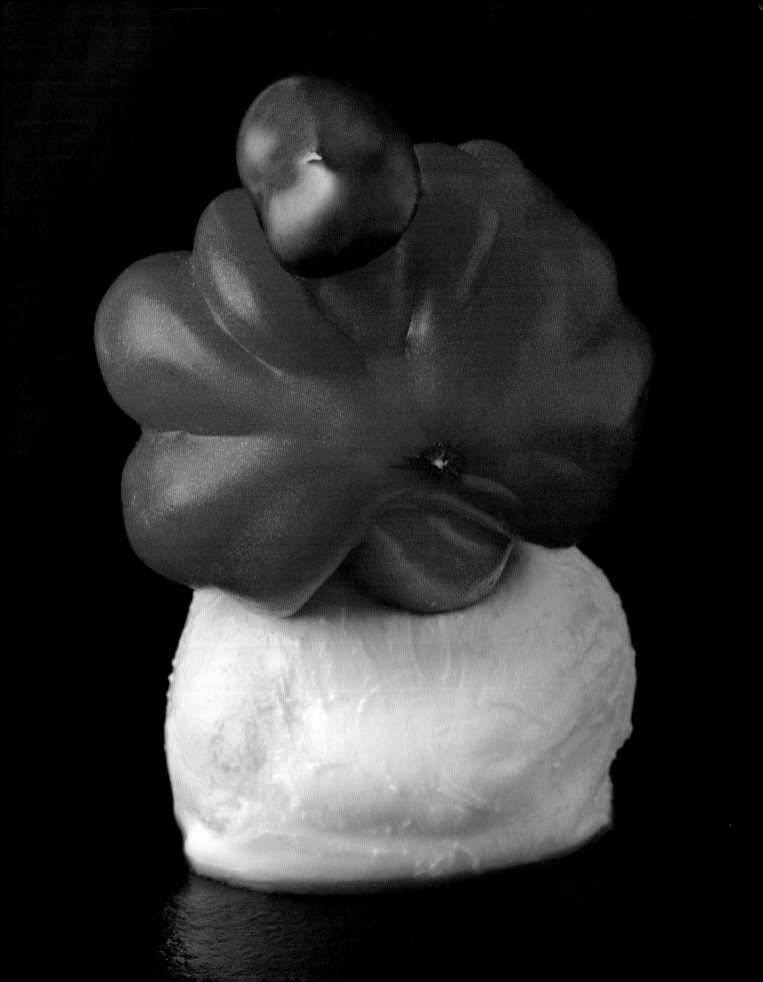

...RIVER CAFÉ CHOCOLATES...

We had the enormous pleasure and privilege of working with Ruth Rogers and the late Rose Gray, founders of the River Café, to create a chocolate together. The chocolate we worked on is sublime in so many ways. Rose and Ruth were very specific about using Italian unsalted butter, and also about using chocolate produced by Amedei, a company in Tuscany that makes incredibly fine-quality chocolate. We use Amedei 9, which is made with beans from nine plantations.

Makes 50

30g liquid glucose
15g full-fat milk
160g double cream
200g Amedei 9 chocolate, finely
  chopped
30g unsalted butter, cut into small
  cubes
tempered dark chocolate, for dipping
  (see pages 32–33)
good-quality unsweetened cocoa
  powder, for dusting

Put the glucose, milk and cream in a small pan and bring to the boil. Remove from the heat.

Put the chopped chocolate in a bowl and add the hot cream. Stir gently from the middle to emulsify. Check on a digital thermometer that the temperature is no higher than 45°C, then stir in the butter until combined. Leave in a cool place until firm enough to pipe.

Just before piping, lightly whisk the ganache. Fit a plain 15mm nozzle in a piping bag and fill the bag with the mixture. Pipe 3cm lengths on a baking sheet lined with baking parchment. Leave the piped ganache in a cool place (but not the fridge) for at least 6 hours or overnight to set.

Using a dipping fork, coat the pieces in tempered chocolate then dust lightly with cocoa powder to finish (see page 43).

...pure and simple...

...MICHAEL'S CHOCOLATE FONDANTS...

Michael's arm features quite significantly in this book (see pages 80–81). A talented chocolatier at Melt, he is originally from Australia. Here we share his delicious fondant recipe.

Serves 4

210g dark chocolate, chopped
110g unsalted butter, cut into cubes
2 organic eggs
2 organic egg yolks
95g golden caster sugar
30g good-quality unsweetened cocoa
  powder, plus extra for dusting
35g plain flour

Butter four 100ml ramekins and dust with a little cocoa powder, turning the dishes to coat them and then tipping out any excess.

Put the chocolate and butter in a large heatproof bowl and place in a low oven (about 50°C) for 10–15 minutes, until melted, stirring gently once or twice. Remove and set aside. Increase the oven temperature to 180°C/Gas Mark 4.

Meanwhile, place the eggs, egg yolks and sugar in a bowl and whisk with a handheld electric beater until pale and fluffy. Fold the egg and sugar mixture gently into the melted chocolate and butter. Sift the cocoa powder and flour over the top and gently fold in with a spatula.

Divide the mixture between the prepared ramekins and bake for 10–12 minutes.

Remove from the oven. As soon as they are cool enough to handle, gently run a clean knife around the outside of each fondant to release it from the dish, being careful not to damage the delicate crust. Turn the fondants out on to serving plates – they should just hold their shape.

They are delicious served with crème fraîche, which helps cut through the richness, or clotted cream – for a full-on experience. Serve immediately. Fondants wait for no one!

...STAR BISCUITS...

These biscuits make chic edible decorations. They are exceptionally easy to make and suitable for very little ones to join in with the cooking. We like to make them at Christmas time and hang them on the tree.

Makes about 28

185g unsalted butter
225g vanilla sugar, or 225g caster sugar
  and 1$\frac{1}{2}$ teaspoons vanilla extract
340g plain flour
1 organic egg
1 organic egg yolk
150g milk chocolate
150g dark chocolate
150g white chocolate
silver confectionery balls, to decorate

Place the butter and sugar (and vanilla extract, if using) in a food processor and blend until well mixed. Add the flour, egg and egg yolk and process again until smooth. Wrap in baking parchment and chill in the fridge for at least 30 minutes.

Preheat the oven to 180°C/Gas Mark 4.

Roll out the dough on a flour-dusted work surface until it is 5mm thick, then use a star-shaped cutter to cut out biscuits. Use a skewer to make a hole in each star for a ribbon once cooked. Place the biscuits on baking trays lined with baking parchment and bake for 10 minutes or until pale golden. Transfer to a wire rack to cool. Reduce the oven temperature to 50°C.

Chop or break up the chocolate and put it in 3 separate heatproof bowls. Place in the oven and leave for 10–15 minutes, until melted, stirring gently once or twice. Dip the cooled biscuits into the melted chocolate and place them on baking parchment to set (not on a plate or they will stick). While the chocolate is still molten, scatter liberally with silver balls. The stars can be placed in the fridge for about 10 minutes for the chocolate to set – just in case your helpers get impatient!

Thread ribbon through the holes and hang the biscuits on your Christmas tree. Or, if giving as a present, store in an airtight container for up to a week to keep them crisp.

...pure and simple...

...CHOCOLATE CAKE WITH MASCARPONE AND WHITE CHOCOLATE TOPPING...

The topping for this dark chocolate cake is a very firm favourite in Louise's family. It has topped and filled many, many cakes, particularly birthday cakes, often decorated with a toy animal or two. If you add a little milk or dark chocolate to the mix you can create a 'muddy field' with a horse galloping across – perfect for eight-year-old girls. Double the quantities for the topping if you want to make a large cake, or if you wish to fill and top it.

150g dark chocolate (60 per cent cocoa solids), chopped
175g self-raising flour
1 teaspoon baking powder
175g very soft unsalted butter
175g golden caster sugar
3 organic eggs

For the mascarpone and white chocolate topping
250g white chocolate, chopped
500g mascarpone cheese
150ml double cream

Butter an 18cm round cake tin and dust it lightly with flour.

Put the chopped dark chocolate in a heatproof bowl and place in a low oven (about 50°C) for about 15 minutes, until melted, stirring gently once or twice. Remove from the oven and set aside. Increase the oven temperature to 180°C/Gas Mark 4.

Sift the flour and baking powder into a bowl. Add the butter, sugar and eggs and mix well with a handheld electric beater until completely smooth. Stir in the melted chocolate. Pour the mixture into the prepared tin and bake for 25–30 minutes, until it is well risen and a skewer inserted in the centre comes out clean. Reduce the oven temperature to 50°C. Leave the cake in the tin for 10 minutes, then turn out on to a wire rack to cool.

To prepare the topping, put the white chocolate in a heatproof bowl and place in the oven for about 15 minutes, until melted, stirring occasionally. Keep an eye on it; white chocolate can burn and when it does it goes into small, caramelised lumps – delicious, but not right for now!

While the chocolate is melting, whisk the mascarpone and cream together until well combined. Allow the melted chocolate to cool slightly, then stir it into the cream and mascarpone. The resulting topping is stunning – matt white and not too sweet. When the cake is cool, liberally dollop the topping over it.

spiky

Makes 60

160g dark chocolate (64–70 per cent
    cocoa solids), finely chopped
230g double cream
15g full-fat milk
20g liquid glucose
25g unsalted butter, cut into small
    cubes
60 dark chocolate shells (see page 43)
tempered dark chocolate, for rolling
    (see pages 32–33)

Put the chopped chocolate in a bowl.
Put the cream, milk and glucose in a
small pan and bring just to boiling point,
then remove from the heat and pour on
to the chocolate. Stir gently from the
middle to emulsify. Check on a digital
thermometer that the temperature is no
higher than 45°C, then stir in the butter
until combined.

Leave the mixture to cool to body
temperature, then transfer to a
disposable piping bag, snip off the
tip and pipe into the chocolate shells.
Seal the shells with tempered dark
chocolate, then roll them in the
chocolate (see page 43).

To get a spiky finish, place the dipped
chocolates on a wire cake rack and
wait until the coating is semi-set. Then
use a dipping fork to turn them until
spiky all over – the chocolate will catch
on the grid of the cake rack to create
this effect.

dark

These bonbons have a silky texture.
The ganache is piped into a shell, which
requires a certain dexterity and patience
but will give you a more professional result.
The spiky finish is fun to do, and as we think
fun is an important part of chocolate making
we often include it in our practical tasting
sessions and events. Children especially
love doing the spiky part!

...COLOMBIAN TRUFFLES...

We worked on this recipe with Skye Gyngell of Petersham Nurseries Café and the finished result is punchy and characterful. Skye was very keen for us to use a particular Colombian chocolate that is both grown and produced in its country of origin – very unusual in the chocolate industry. The producers, Santander, have strong ethical credentials and even help to fund and run a school. If you have trouble getting hold of their chocolate, choose a dark, intense chocolate with at least 70 per cent cocoa solids, such as Valrhona's Abinao 85% or Guanaja 70%, or Melt's Wine Bar. The saltiness from the organic butter balances very well with the strong, dark Colombian chocolate, rich in coffee notes.

Makes 50

140g Colombian chocolate (70 per cent cocoa solids), finely chopped
125g double cream
35g full-fat milk
30g liquid glucose
35g organic salted butter, cut into cubes
50 square dark chocolate cups (see page 43)
tempered dark chocolate, for dipping (see pages 32–33)
good-quality unsweetened cocoa powder, for dusting

Put the chopped chocolate in a bowl. Put the cream, milk and glucose in a small pan and bring just to boiling point, then remove from the heat and pour on to the chocolate. Stir gently from the middle to emulsify. Check on a digital thermometer that the temperature is no higher than 45°C, then stir in the butter until combined.

Set aside to cool to body temperature. Pipe the mixture into the chocolate cups and leave in a cool place (but not the fridge) for at least 6 hours or overnight to set.

Use a dipping fork, coat the truffles in tempered chocolate, then dust with sifted cocoa powder to finish (see page 43).

...pure and simple...

...BABIES' KISSES...

This is a version of the Italian *baci di dama* – very simple to make and with the sometimes necessary benefit of containing no nuts and no eggs. They are super light, with a real melt-in-the-mouth texture. The biscuits are so beautifully fragile that you have to spoon the ganache filling on to them rather than spreading it; use the ganache when it has set to unripe-Camembert stage. You could play around and use a variety of flavoured ganaches – see pages 37–39.

162

Makes about 30

200g unsalted butter, softened
50g icing sugar
2 teaspoons good-quality vanilla extract
300g self-raising flour
1 quantity of Chocolate Ganache (see page 37), chilled for 1 hour

Preheat the oven to 180°C/Gas Mark 4. Line a baking tray with baking parchment.

Place the butter, icing sugar and vanilla extract in a bowl and beat with a handheld electric beater until really pale in colour. Sift the flour over the mixture and combine well using the electric beater – the mixture should come together into a dough.

Make small balls of the dough about 2–3cm in diameter (they will spread to 3–4cm when cooked) and place on the lined baking tray. Flatten slightly with a fork – this creates an attractive pattern. I sometimes use a handheld aerolatte (a tool that whisks milk for coffee) to do this.

Bake the biscuits for 10 minutes or until they are golden brown. Leave to cool on the baking tray and then sandwich together with the ganache. Eat within 48 hours.

...CHOCOLATE-DIPPED FINANCIERS...

These little French almond cakes are traditionally baked in small, rectangular moulds but we think madeleine moulds give a prettier shape. They are perfect for a fast and fabulous dessert, served with double cream and fresh raspberries. This recipe is a great way of using up excess egg whites after an ice-cream-making frenzy. In fact, it is worth making ice cream simply to have the whites left over in order to do this recipe, which is sure to become a firm favourite. If you have time, try grinding whole, unskinned almonds in a food processor – it gives a more pleasing, non-uniform texture.

Makes about 24

170g unsalted butter, plus 30g for
 greasing the moulds
55g plain flour
135g ground almonds
250g golden caster sugar
5 organic egg whites
200g dark chocolate (at least 60 per
 cent cocoa solids), finely chopped
icing sugar, for dusting

Preheat the oven to 240°C/Gas Mark 9. Melt the 30g of butter for greasing and use to brush two 12-hole madeleine moulds.

Melt the 170g butter in a small pan and let it bubble until it starts to brown a touch and smells wonderfully nutty. Remove from the heat and let it cool a little.

Sift the flour into a bowl and stir in the ground almonds and sugar. Stir in the egg whites vigorously to form a sticky paste. Pour in the melted butter and stir well until the ingredients are thoroughly combined. Divide the mixture evenly between the moulds, filling them to just below the rim.

Bake for 5 minutes, then reduce the oven temperature to 200°C/Gas Mark 6 and bake for a further 5 minutes. Finally, leave in the switched-off oven for a final 5 minutes. Remove from the oven and, using a paring knife, gently ease the financiers out of the moulds – work fairly quickly as they start to stick if left too long. Leave the financiers to cool on a wire rack.

Place the chopped-up chocolate in a heatproof bowl and leave in the turned-off oven for about 10 minutes, until melted. Dip the financiers into the molten chocolate and leave on baking parchment until set. Finish with a generous dusting of icing sugar.

...pure and simple...

...CHOCOLATE MACAROONS...

Shop-bought macaroons have a tendency to be far too sweet and powdery. However, since we make ours in a small kitchen with a domestic oven, as you would at home, and not on an industrial scale, we think Melt macaroons have more depth. We fill them with a really thick layer of ganache, which is utterly delectable.

164

Makes about 80

250g ground almonds
250g icing sugar
45g good-quality unsweetened cocoa powder
210g organic egg whites
250g caster sugar
75g water

For the ganache
290g dark chocolate (66 per cent cocoa solids), finely chopped
250g double cream
70g milk
60g liquid glucose
70g unsalted butter, cut into cubes

Put the ground almonds, icing sugar and cocoa powder in a food processor and whizz until fine and lump free. Transfer to a large bowl.

Measure out 105g of the egg whites, add to the ground almond mixture and stir until you have a paste. Set aside. Put the remaining 105g egg whites in the bowl of a freestanding electric mixer fitted with the whisk attachment.

Put the caster sugar and water in a small, heavy-based pan and bring slowly to the boil, stirring to dissolve the sugar. Boil, without stirring, until it reaches 118°C on a sugar thermometer. Shortly before it reaches this temperature, start whisking the egg whites on medium speed, just to aerate them. Slowly pour in the sugar syrup down the side of the bowl, whisking all the time. After the sugar syrup has all been added, continue to whisk on medium speed until the mixture forms stiff peaks; it should be at body temperature.

Add about half the meringue to the ground almond mixture and fold in roughly to loosen it. Quickly mix in the remaining meringue until just combined; be careful not to overwork it or it will become too loose.

Transfer the mixture to a piping bag fitted with an 8mm nozzle. Pipe it into 2.5cm rounds on to baking sheets lined with baking parchment or silicone baking mats. Lightly tap each baking sheet on the work surface a few times to smooth the top of the macaroons. Leave to stand for 30 minutes, until slightly dry to the touch. Preheat the oven to 130°C/Gas Mark ³/₄.

Bake the macaroons for 10–15 minutes – lift one off the paper to check if they're done; it should come off with only a little resistance. If your macaroons have succeeded perfectly, each one will have a little frilly section at the base – this is known as the 'foot'. Remove the baking parchment or silicone mats from the trays, complete with macaroons, and leave on a work surface to cool completely.

Meanwhile, make the ganache. Put the chocolate in a bowl. Place the cream, milk and glucose in a small pan and heat to boiling point, then pour on to the chocolate. Stir from the middle to emulsify. Check on a digital thermometer that the temperature is no higher than 45°C, then gently mix in the butter. Leave in a cool place until firm enough to pipe.

Carefully peel the macaroons off the paper. Match them up into pairs of equal size. Put the ganache in a piping bag fitted with an 8mm nozzle and pipe on to the flat side of half the macaroons, then sandwich them together with their matching halves. They are best left in the fridge overnight before serving, but bring them to room temperature before you eat them.

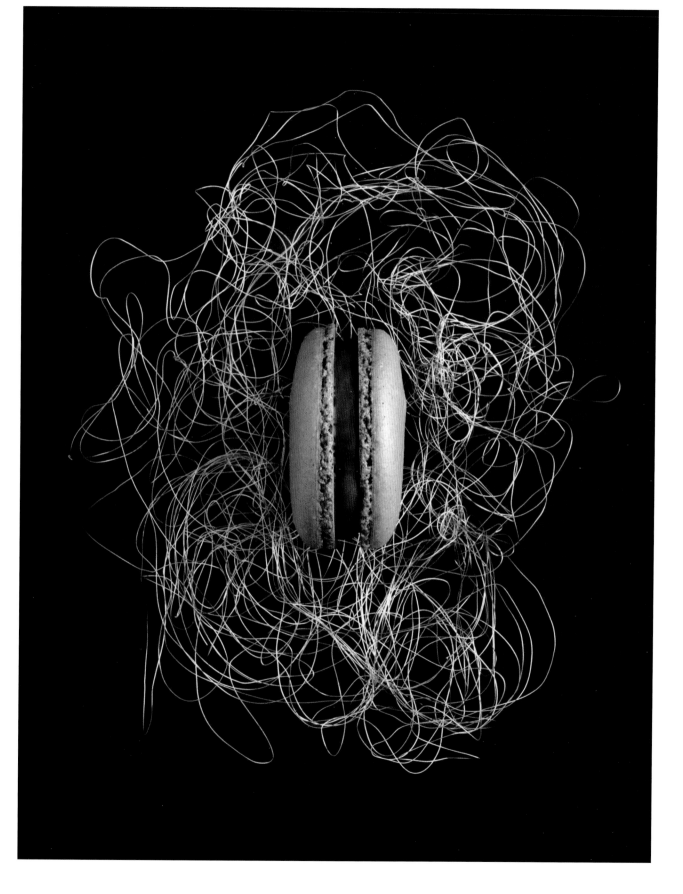

...ki*ck!*...

...HOJI TEA BONBONS...

Hoji, or hojicha, is a Japanese green tea roasted in a porcelain pot over charcoal. It's a popular tea to serve with a meal or at bedtime. We decorate these bonbons with genmai tea, which is green tea combined with roasted brown rice. Sometimes called 'popcorn tea', because the rice grains resemble popcorn, it makes a really attractive and unusual finish.

Makes 50

200g water
15g hoji tea leaves
110g milk chocolate (40 per cent cocoa solids), finely chopped
40g dark chocolate (at least 64 per cent cocoa solids), finely chopped
15g liquid glucose
25g unsalted butter, cut into small cubes
50 square dark chocolate cups (see page 43)
tempered dark chocolate, for dipping (see pages 32–33)
tea leaves, preferably genmai tea, to decorate

Heat the water to 80°C in a small pan, add the hoji tea leaves and leave to infuse for 6 hours. Strain the tea.

Put the milk chocolate and dark chocolate in a bowl. Bring the infused water to the boil again with the glucose and pour it over the chocolate. Stir gently from the middle to emulsify. Check on a digital thermometer that the temperature is no higher than 45°C, then stir in the butter until combined. Set aside to cool to body temperature.

Pour the cooled mixture into the chocolate cups. Set aside in a cool place (but not the fridge) for at least 6 hours or overnight for the filling to firm up.

Dip the chocolates in the tempered dark chocolate (see page 43) and sprinkle a few tea leaves on top to decorate.

...MARC DE CHAMPAGNE BONBONS...

Contrary to what you might think, a classic champagne truffle is made not with bubbly champagne but with marc de champagne, a brandy produced from the grape skins left over from the initial stages of champagne production. Champagne truffles can vary enormously in quality – at worst sweet and sickly, at best refined and luxurious. These fall into the latter category.

Makes 50

165g milk chocolate (40 per cent cocoa solids), finely chopped
150g white chocolate (35 per cent cocoa solids), finely chopped
150g double cream
15g full-fat milk
45g liquid glucose
50g marc de champagne
50 dark chocolate shells (see page 43)
tempered dark chocolate, for rolling (see pages 32–33)
icing sugar, for dusting

Put the milk chocolate and white chocolate in a bowl. Put the cream, milk and glucose in a small pan and bring just to boiling point. Remove from the heat and pour on to the chocolate, then stir gently from the middle to emulsify. Check on a digital thermometer that the temperature is no higher than 45°C, then stir in the marc de champagne until combined. Leave to cool to body temperature.

Snip the end off a disposable piping bag to leave a 3mm hole. Fill the bag with the ganache and pipe into the chocolate shells.

Seal the shells with tempered dark chocolate, then roll them in the chocolate to coat (see page 43). Dust with icing sugar and leave to set.

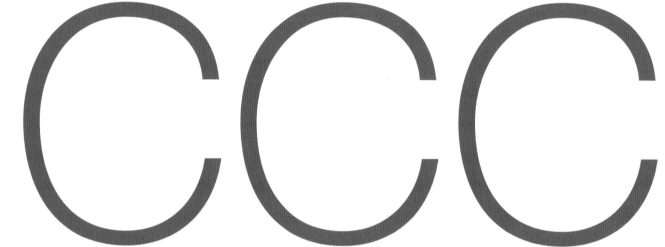

Cardamom has a very distinctive flavour that is absolutely wonderful infused in cream and made into a ganache. The balance has to be perfect though, otherwise it will overpower the subtle nuances of the chocolate. The addition of coffee makes this a very sophisticated chocolate.

...COFFEE CARDAMOM CUPS...

Makes 50

175g double cream
15g full-fat milk
10g liquid glucose
1 teaspoon ground espresso coffee,
  plus a pinch to decorate
10 cardamom seeds, roughly crushed
175g milk chocolate (35–40 per cent
  cocoa solids), finely chopped
20g unsalted butter, cut into small
  cubes
50 dark chocolate cups (see page 43)
tempered dark chocolate, for sealing
  (see pages 32–33)

Place the double cream, milk, glucose, coffee and cardamom seeds in a small pan, bring to the boil, then remove from the heat and leave to infuse for 30 minutes.

Put the chopped chocolate in a bowl. Pour the infused cream through a fine sieve into a clean pan, bring to the boil again and pour it over the chocolate. Stir gently from the middle to emulsify. Check on a digital thermometer that the temperature is no higher than 45°C, then stir in the butter until well combined. Set the mixture aside to cool to body temperature.

Pour the ganache into the chocolate cups. Set aside in a cool place (but not the fridge) to firm up.

Seal the chocolates with the tempered dark chocolate (see page 43) and sprinkle a little coffee powder on top to decorate.

...kick...

...SOPHIE CONRAN'S EARL GREY, CRANBERRY AND GINGER CHOCOLATES...

The Armagnac, prune and ginger pie in Sophie Conran's book, *Pies* (HarperCollins, 2006), was the inspiration for this wonderful, quirky chocolate. It is fabulous and just a little bit eccentric. We loved working with Sophie, who is very approachable and has a great eye for design. She chose the most wonderful, vibrant orange box to go with the chocolates – the combination was stunning.

Make 50

180g double cream
10g full-fat milk
20g liquid glucose
7g Earl Grey tea leaves
180g dark chocolate (at least 60 per cent cocoa solids), finely chopped
25g unsalted butter, cut into small cubes
50 small pieces of crystallised ginger
50 dark chocolate cups (see page 43)
tempered dark chocolate, for sealing (see pages 32–33)
50 dried cranberries, to decorate

Place the double cream, milk and glucose in a small pan, bring to the boil and then remove from the heat. Add the Earl Grey tea and set aside to infuse for 30 minutes.

Put the chopped chocolate in a bowl. Strain the cream through a fine sieve into a clean pan, bring to the boil again and then pour it over the chocolate. Stir gently from the middle to emulsify. Check on a digital thermometer that the temperature is no higher than 45°C, then stir in the butter until well combined. Set aside to cool to body temperature.

Put a piece of crystallised ginger in each chocolate cup, then pour in the ganache. Set aside in a cool place (but not the fridge) for at least 6 hours or overnight for the filling to firm up.

Seal the chocolates with the tempered dark chocolate (see page 43) and place a dried cranberry on top to decorate.

...kick...

...SEA SALT CARAMELS...

This is one of the most popular chocolates in our repertoire. The contrast in textures is one of the reasons it is such a star. First there is the crunch of a thick layer of dark chocolate, followed by oozing caramel, then you are greeted by a sticky sweetness with a hint of bitterness, closely followed by sea salt. We use the British sea salt, Maldon, which has wonderful large crystals.

176

Makes 60

250g double cream
35g milk
seeds from ¹/₂ vanilla pod
4g sea salt
50g liquid glucose
250g caster sugar
25g unsalted butter, cut into cubes
60 dark chocolate shells (see page 43)
tempered dark chocolate, for rolling
   (see pages 32–33)
300g good-quality unsweetened cocoa
   powder, for dusting

Put the cream, milk, vanilla seeds and sea salt in a small pan, bring just to boiling point, then remove from the heat and set aside.

Put the glucose in a heavy-based pan and place over a high heat. When it begins to bubble, add a little sugar and stir until melted. Keep adding the sugar until it is all used up, then raise the heat and boil without stirring until you have a golden brown caramel. Remove from the heat, add the warm cream mixture and stir until smooth. Stir in the butter until completely combined, then leave to cool. Pipe the mixture into the chocolate shells.

Seal the shells with tempered dark chocolate, then roll them in the chocolate to coat (see page 43). Dust with cocoa powder (see page43) and leave to set.

...SALTED PRALINES...

This recipe is Louise's daughter Kitty's all-time favourite. She will rummage around in the little Melt paper bag to fish out this star of a chocolate. The partnership of nuts and salt is so well recognised in our taste memory bank, and it is just wonderful combined with dark chocolate. If you don't place the hazelnut on top in time, it won't stick. It is these 'rejects' at Melt that are highly sought after by the staff.

Makes 50

650g smooth praline paste
6g sea salt
50 dark chocolate cups (see page 43)
tempered dark chocolate, for sealing
   (see pages 32–33)
50 hazelnuts, to decorate

Put the praline and sea salt in a bowl and mix very well.

Snip the tip off a disposable piping bag to leave a 3mm hole. Fill the bag with the praline mixture and pipe it into the chocolate cups.

Seal the cups with tempered dark chocolate (see page 43), then put a hazelnut on top of each one and leave to set.

supp.
i
than

liers

ier

ndex

k you.

...SUPPLIERS...

Since setting up Melt several years ago, sourcing supplies for chocolate equipment and packaging has become much easier. If only it had been as advanced when we started as it is now! The internet has brought the world to our fingertips, and now even the smallest suppliers usually have a website. It's sometimes worth having a look around websites in the United States, China and Italy. We source items such as sugar decorations from the States because they do particularly good ones, but be aware that shipping tends to be very expensive.

There are two main types of suppliers for chocolate and chocolate-making equipment: trade and retail use. Unless you are thinking of taking chocolate to a business level, it's not really worth dealing with all the trade-related documents and large minimum-order quantities. There are some great online companies selling all you need in smaller quantities – we used lots of these suppliers when we were experimenting and just starting out at Melt. You should be able to get everything you need to make the recipes in this book from the companies listed opposite.

Chocolate-making equipment and ingredients

Chocolat at Home
www.chocolatathome.com
Based in Belgium (so do check the delivery charges), Chocolat at Home provides all the essentials for chocolate making in small quantities: chocolate shells, praline paste, disposable piping bags, dipping forks – and, of course, good chocolate! They also sell beginner's chocolate kits containing everything you need to get started.

Healthy Supplies
www.healthysupplies.co.uk
Predominantly a healthfood supplier, this company stocks freeze-dried whole and powdered fruit, such as raspberries, strawberries, blackberries and bananas, at very competitive prices.

Home Chocolate Factory
www.homechocolatefactory.com
A comprehensive range of chocolate and chocolate-making equipment – moulds, chocolate shells, transfer sheets and much more.

Infusions 4 Chefs Ltd
www.infusions4chefs.co.uk
Suppliers of speciality ingredients to chefs, including cocoa nibs, praline paste, dried lemon verbena leaves and fruit purées.

Keylink

www.keylink.org

Popular with many professionals, this supplier stocks a vast range of chocolate products, specialist equipment and packaging, plus fruit purées, flavourings and freeze-dried fruit. Some items are only available in large quantities, and there is a fairly hefty delivery charge for small orders, but its prices are very competitive.

Make a Wish!

www.makeawishcakeshop.co.uk

Although this is primarily a cake-decorating business, it stocks crystallised mint leaves, rose petals and violets – useful for chocolate making.

Melt

www.meltchocolates.com

We offer chocolate-making equipment, chocolate shells and cups, cocoa nibs etc through our online shop. If you cannot find what you need on our website, do send us an email and we will endeavour to supply it.

The Spicery

www.thespicery.com

Grinds and blends spices in small batches to maximise freshness. Also stocks dried lemon verbena leaves, rosebuds and petals, tonka beans and a selection of luscious vanilla pods.

Squires Kitchen

www.squires-shop.com

Sells chocolate and chocolate-making equipment, including a wide assortment of polycarbonate and silicone chocolate moulds. Also sells feuilletine and cocoa butter in small quantities, useful for home chocolatiers.

Chocolate information and discussions

Academy of Chocolate

www.academyofchocolate.org.uk

Based in the UK, the Academy aims to encourage chocolate lovers to 'look beyond the label' and learn to appreciate fine chocolate. It also encourages sustainable cocoa production and transparent sourcing of cocoa beans.

International Cocoa Organisation

www.icco.org

A global organisation that promotes sustainable cocoa production and consumption.

Seventypercent.com

www.seventypercent.com

A chocolate appreciation site full of chocolate reviews and discussions, run by enthusiasts 'with more time than sense and a fairly harmless addiction'.

World Cocoa Foundation

www.worldcocoafoundation.org

Founded in 2000 to promote social and economic development and environmental stewardship in cocoa-growing countries.

...INDEX...

185

...index...

thank you

From Louise

I would like to give a huge thank you to Jean Cazals, without whom this book would not have happened. His sheer energy, drive and passion have been a beacon throughout. Every photograph could tell a story!

192

This book would also not have been possible without the great support, patience and input from Jon Croft and Matt Inwood at Absolute Press, and the book's editor, Jane Middleton.

Every day, I used to call my mother 'the best cook in the whole wide world'. Her brilliant cooking has influenced me enormously. She also gave me chocolate cookbooks at the tender age of eight.

Thank you also to my mother-in-law, Anne, who did early proofreading to correct my terrible spelling!

The biggest thank you has to go to my four children, Charlie, Charlotte, Kitty and Ben, who are constantly and unwaveringly fascinated and excited by Melt and had many an opinion and idea for both the book and its recipes.

And, of course, to my loving husband, Andrew, who happily ate his way through all the recipes.

From Chika

I'd like to thank Jean Cazals for his passion and amazing creativity and complete love of chocolate! I'd also like to thank Jane Middleton for being fantastic at working through my notes and technical chocolate recipes. Finally, I'd like to thank the Melt team, for whom creativity and deliciousness are priorities.

...melt...